Girlfriend from Hades

by

Christopher Smith

©2010-2012

Published by SRE Publishing

Copyright © 2010-2012 by Christopher Smith

All Rights Reserved.

No part of this publication may be reproduced, stored in a retrieval system, or transmitted in any form or by any means, electronic, mechanical, photocopying, recording, or otherwise, without written permission of the author.

Published in the United States by SRE Publishing.

www.lifewithhades.com
www.girlfriendfromhades.com

ISBN-13: 978-0615515977
ISBN-10: 0615515975

First Edition: February 2012

Cover photo by Christopher Smith

For questions or comments regarding this book, email the author at girlfriend.from.hades@gmail.com

Based on True Events

Thank you for buying my book.

For those of you in an unhealthy relationship,
it only gets worse.

TABLE OF CONTENTS

You Need a Strong Antagonist.................... 1

Honesty in the Form of Lies....................... 3

Maybe She Was Just a Sociopath................ 5

Ain't Nothin' But a G Thing, Baby............... 8

How I Spent My Easter Vacation................ 10

I Love You, Drugs, and Alcohol (But Not Necessarily in that Order)..................... 13

A Different Kind of Courtship..................... 16

Bless This Mess... 19

Tag, You're It!.. 22

Let's Get Laid... 24

The G Spot... 26

Nice Ink.. 30

Adderall and All for One............................. 33

Can I Get Some Fries with that Shake?....... 36

I'll Take "The Rapists" for One Hundred, Alex... 42

My Sink Won't Sleep For Weeks.................. 45

Gonna Set My Soul, Gonna Set My Soul On Fire...".. 49

That's What I Like About You..................... 53

I Take Two Steps Forward, You Take Two Steps Back..55

A Thug is a Thug is a Thug............................ 58

In Memoriam.................................. 61

… --- 65

How Are Ya? How Are Ya? How Are Ya?.... 69

The Man, The Myth, The Legend.................. 72

The 61 Reasons.. 75

Highway to Hell...80

Going 101 South..84

Dearly Departed.. 87

Art is Art is Art...90

Her Cup Runneth Over...................................92

Insane in the Membrane............................... 95

The Passenger.. 99

Good Mourning!... 103

6 Months, Time Served................................. 106

Keyless Entry... 109

Failure to Launch (Part I)............................ 113

Failure to Launch (Part II)........................... 116

Cantaloupe.. 120

Betting Against the House............................ 123

Numerology FTW!.. 126

"Did You Eat Any Rotten Food?" (Vegas, Part II).. 129

Say, "Cheese!" (Vegas, Part III)...................... 132

A House of Cards... 134

The Streets of San Francisco......................... 137

Are You Listening?... 140

This Ends Here... Maybe?............................. 144

Quitters Never Win, Winners Never Quit..... 147

You're Pathological... 151

Hop On In, I'll Get Ya There........................... 156

Lying on the Beach... 160

Date Night... 162

E=mc2.. 165

Four Word Question; One Word Answer....... 168

Two Tired.. 170

Art Show... 172

If You Lived Here, You'd Be Home Right Now... 175

For Medicinal Purposes Only......................... 179

I'm Ready For My Close-Up........................... 181

Shattered: Literally and Figuratively.......... 183

Blood on my Hands... 187

And the Band Played On................................ 189

Pain in the Neck... 191

I N F P... 193

Give Thanks.. 195

HOA.. 197

Medical, Dental, and Vision.......................... 199

Cloudy Days Ahead.. 202

We Need to Talk.. 204

Superficially Wounded................................... 206

Better to Give... 209

The Ghost of Christmas Past........................ 211

Smile... 213

Coupling.. 215

365 Days of This.. 218

Crack Pipes... 221

Speaks for Itself.. 224

East Coast Friend... 225

Monkeying Around... 228

The We Dog.. 230

Seize Her!	234
Mailbag	237
All the Best	239
Unpainted Corner	240
V-D	244
[		]	246
Rx for Trouble	249
Doctoring the Day	253
Pandora's Box	257
Pandora's Phone	260
Forked	263
Dad	266
Long Weekend	269
Infidel	274
Take Notes	277
Abort Mission	282
The Calm Before	287
The Storm	290
Strangers	293
The Picture of Success!	296
Cut the Strings	305

I Am Over It... 309

I Don't Float.. 312

Closing Credits.. 315

Glossary of Terms...317

Girlfriend from Hades

Introduction

I've heard the rules before. Write what you know, but never, ever write too personally about something, especially a relationship... other people's relationships are boring to anyone but the two people in them, and even sometimes are not even interesting to those that lived through it.

Here I am, breaking the rules. I know I'm not exempt from it, and I know my life is probably no more interesting that the next person. In fact, for the most part, I feel like I lead a pretty normal life, free from anything close to drama. Anything above that gets regurgitated to my therapist over and over again.

This situation was different, at least it was for me. Fourteen months is not a long time, and here I am finally adding an introduction long after it was over, in fact, this is the last part I am writing to this book. For me, that year and two months, I was what I call "Miserably in

Love." I never imagined feeling so connected to someone that was so above and beyond help that she became completely and utterly self-destructive. The black hole was so deep, I was inadvertently allowing myself to be sucked right in.

I never thought I would craft a book from all this. This all began as a blog with the same name, "Girlfriend from Hades." It was, more or less, a way for me to not just cope with a heavy hearted break-up, but to also relay what happened to friends and family so I wouldn't have to tell it over and over and over again. The blog was cathartic and while helped with the healing at first, most certainly hindered that later on. Once I started, I didn't want to leave the story unfinished, which drew out this break-up much longer than necessary. When you have a bad break-up, everything should be left in the past, or as it's said on the internet: hit the gym, delete Facebook, and lawyer up.

As I wrote, my intention was to exercise all the demons and resentment I held within. Then something strange happened: I received a email thanking me. As it turns out, there are others in my situation that feel stuck. One email turned into two, two into four and so on. People from around the world were able to relate to this relationship.

With that, I decided to publish this for anyone and everyone that may need a little bit of guidance or to just laugh at my expense.

CHAPTER 1
You Need a Strong Antagonist

In movies, it's always said, "Your hero is only as strong as your villain." Look at your classics: Star Wars had Darth Vader, Superman had Lex Luthor (or Zod if you love Superman II as much as I do), Die Hard had Hans Gruber, and Harry Potter had Voldemort. If your protagonist can thwart those antagonists, then they are stronger, badder, and more bitchin' than ever.

Like all stories, this one starts at the beginning and involves a pretty girl that I now refer to by the name *Hades*. She appeared normal in every way, but inside lurked an evil that took over a year to finally see and understand. She was one or all of the following: a sufferer of something called Borderline Personality Disorder, a Sociopath, a Pathological Liar, or just born to destroy others.

I saw everything that was going on, but put blinders on because when you date a pathological liar, it's like a paradox: math, science, and logic do not exist in this Twilight Zone and 2 + 2 does some how, in fact, equal 5.

I'm no saint either. I only fueled the fire of my own problems. Her oil to my water did nothing but create an undiscussed reaction that burned under the surface. I am a bit crazy and I too acted in ways someone shouldn't. I was lied to and manipulated and looking back in hindsight only now see the sucker that landed in her crosshairs.

All my life I've heard about "The One That Got Away," but what happens when it's you? I suppose for every one that gets away, there's the one you can't let go of and when the two meet up, this is what happens. Everyone has that *One*, the One that disrupted their life, the One that your friends kept telling you was bad for you, the One that no matter how bad it seemed on paper, was always the One that kept coming back. You tell yourself that things will get better, it's not as bad as people think, and while you may be good for them, you don't see how bad they are for you.

These are the stories of my One. Fourteen months from start to finish. Pages and pages of my own attempt to find the humor while trying to convince myself and others that even if you are the one that gets away from someone else, even if you don't want to go, eventually you will have to.

That said, she was very pretty with a body to over throw countries just to touch again, so it wasn't ALL bad.

CHAPTER 2
Honesty in the Form of Lies

When I first met her, she was beautiful, funny, and above all things: honest. We were meeting for business, but over two glasses of wine, the conversation and mood became more of a good first date... flirtatious, laughter, and really getting to know one another. She told me all about her past, the accident that took her brother's life, the following cocaine addiction, her stint through rehab at 22 (she was now 28), and even her DUI from five months ago.

Was she perfect?
No.

Was she open about everything?
At the time, I would have said yes.

She was an aspiring actress and model, but unlike everyone else in this town, she had so much depth and other interests: photography, writing, poetry, and was even a former gymnast. So what if she was sidetracked for a bit in her early 20's. She still managed to graduate college, experiment with going after her Masters, and seemed more down-to-earth than most people I knew. Plus she made me laugh. Her sense of humor was one of her greatest assets and to this day one of the things I miss most about her.

But, the girl was troubled. As open as she seemed to be, this was just the beginning of opening the onion to find out much bigger issues than just a one-time coke addiction. She was a master manipulator and for some reason I was her next target. She would pretend to be all things that I wanted and everything out of her mouth was perfect, however, actions do speak louder than words and her actions were deafening. Too bad it took me so long to listen.

CHAPTER 3
Maybe She Was Just a Sociopath

I always knew she had mental problems. She lied without remorse and even when caught she would deny the truth and then go cry for sympathy or pity. One time I caught her in a pretty big lie. Her alibi just accidentally sold her out. On the way home I simply asked her, "Why do you lie to me?" and she coldly said back, "Because it's easier." It was about the eighth time my brain said, "Get out!" but she continued to charm me and twist the situation back on me.

We talked more about it throughout the night. She reasoned that she lied because it was a trait she learned from her mom. She was always told to keep life happy and if it was easier and kept the situation "happy" then go ahead and lie. She even asked if I would get on the phone with her sister so she too could explain how they were raised. I agreed.

Hades brilliantly turned things around and even when she was completely at fault for something, she knew just how to make you doubt yourself. To be fair, I never wanted to be with someone that was untrustworthy or had these kinds of problems, so I always wanted to believe what she told me was the truth.

The next afternoon, for about 20 minutes, her sister warned me that she would always lie to me. That she would never stop and that it would take years of therapy before my girlfriend would ever change (if she was even capable of change.)

When something bothered me, I usually held it in, tried to look at the big picture. Was my gut feeling right? I can't just make an accusation without proof. Whereas, when something bothered her, she struck hard and fast. I can't even recall the amount of calls I would receive in the middle of the night about something that bothered her that was meritless. When this happened, I knew it was the Borderline in her talking, and tried to make everything better. If I did the same thing, she would breakdown and cry until she eventually shut down. Accusations would get nowhere except the guilt trip for making them, therefore my reaction quickly became that of holding onto it until I knew more.

Sadly this would take over our relationship. Once the trust was broken, there was no going back. Sometimes our conversations would become more Q&A of me looking for cracks in her story, and I think she knew that.

I'm not really sure why at this point I didn't listen. I suppose part of me was mildly brainwashed and/or suffering from some kind of Stockholm Syndrome. In my mind, this girl was various forms of perfect and breaking that illusion would mean I was stuck in the desert. What's worse? Standing strong with your mirage or lost among miles and miles of sand? Whether I wanted to admit it or not, the trust was being eaten away by her deception and no matter how much I wanted to believe her, I wasn't taking a drink from an oasis, but shoveling sand don my throat.

CHAPTER 4
Ain't Nothin' But a G Thing, Baby

Did you know that the date rape drug is taken recreationally? Me neither. Unless you said, "Yes" in which my reply would be, "I had no idea."

I always knew it as "Roofies" or in old timey days it was called a "Mickey." GHB, or as she called it, "G" is a salty liquid known on the rave scene to get a feeling of super-euphoria or I guess it's something known to be slipped into a girl's drink to knock them out. Either way, I didn't know what it was when she first mentioned it. Yes, I had to Wikipedia GHB.

It was shortly after we started dating and one night she was supposed to come over. At some point she ended up at her female-failed-pseudo-rockstar-musician-friend's (FFPRMF) place (a little shanty of an apartment on Fairfax and Melrose). She kept calling me every 20 minutes or so trying to explain why she wasn't with me yet and with each call she was more and more lit. At one point her FFPRMF grabbed the phone to lethargically tell me how much the eventual Girlfriend from Hades liked me.

At some point, around 3am, the FFPRMF told me I should probably come over and get the girl because she was in no condition to drive. I got over there and Hades and FFPRMF were doing some homemade photo shoot. I loaded her into the car, glassy eyes and all, and she said, "I'm sorry... I took G." Other than blatantly being a drug, I had no idea what was in her.

On the way out I noticed she was parked in a tow away zone, so I left her in my car and moved her to a 15-minute meter that would go into effect at 7:00 the next morning, then I drove her to my place. I carried her upstairs and she passed out in my bed. I didn't want her to get towed or get a ticket so I walked in the rain back to her car, moved it to my place and eventually at 5:00 AM I arrived back home to make sure she was still breathing.

This is when I first debated this relationship. I stood in my kitchen in the dark and imagined a pair of scales in front of me: Let her sleep? Throw her out? Let her sleep? Throw her out? The scales moved back and forth and eventually the idea of her driving anywhere decided I would let her sleep. That and a notion my therapist has that as a boyfriend I like to "save girls that need help."

And saving them I do and this book apparently is the pay off.

CHAPTER 5
How I Spent My Easter Vacation

Ah, the joys of Easter. Secular or not, you either have Jesus and the resurrection or the Easter Bunny and chocolates. Last year I spent Easter in the hospital. Thankfully, I wasn't the patient... If I had been, Hades surely wouldn't have been around to take care of me.

In the wee hours of that morning and after Hades had enough to drink to fall somewhere between happy drunk and violent drunk (right on that borderline of fear and love), she broke out a DVD. Like Hades herself, it was as unexpected as one might... expect: the video of her brother's funeral.

Over an hour of friends and family getting in front of everyone to tell stories of someone I had never met except through Hades' tears. Outside of that was her running commentary, "I hate this asshole," "This person should rot in hell, and my favorite, "This guy was caught fucking a dog,"

Her brother's death was tragic and somehow turned what may have been a perfect, happy family into a shred of their former existence. It would be more tragic if Hades didn't use the death to benefit herself: using sob stories to gain sympathy and her dead brother's name to swear she either did or didn't do something. "I swear on _____ name, I am not lying," which of later I would find out she was lying.

After watching her eulogy and as the sun was rising from the East, Hades stood up and threw her wine glass at the wall. The glass shattered, but thankfully it was empty. God forbid she would ever waste a drop of wine. She cried for a few minutes before going out onto the balcony.

I tried to comfort her. I tried to comfort her even more when I saw her sit on the concrete wall separating her and a 15-foot drop. She asked me if I could let her be alone for a few minutes. I contemplated this: Hades was a former gymnast who could do flips, hand stands, and many other things on something no wider than this balcony wall, but she was also drunk. I decided to give her the time it would take for me to go to the bathroom and return. 45 seconds later, I looked out the glass door and saw an empty balcony.

I rushed outside immediately. Looking over, I see Hades laying in the bushes 15 feet below. I ran out the door, down the hall, down the stairs, busting out the main doors of the building to see her motionless body, her head mere inches from a large rock. Was she dead?

As I walked her inside, teetering and tottering, she refused any kind of medical attention. I threatened to call an ambulance (not a new thing in our relationship) but she again refuses. All she wants to do is crawl into bed and go to sleep... I figure that's either because she has been up for 36 hours or maybe it's the possible concussion.

After an hour of fighting, in between me checking her head; the sensation in her limbs, fingers, and toes; and short-term memory, I finally say, "Fuck it," and let her sleep.

5:00pm rolls around, she wakes up and after sitting on the couch for an hour agrees to go to the Emergency Room. Doctor after doctor, nurse after nurse come in and out of her room: none to treat her, most just want to meet the girl that fell off her balcony. She tells them all she woke up early to enjoy an Easter sunrise.

She was admitted, x-rayed, scanned, tested, and tested some more. At first they thought she broke her back (something she had done once before as a gymnast), but that was ruled out and with some pain killers (hooray for her!) she was released at around 2:00am with bruises and the knowledge of a possible underlying chronic back problem, which she would later use to try to get out of community service (another story for another time).

We picked up her prescriptions and went home, but not before stopping at a diner to get a dried out and overdue Easter dinner. Later, Hades, never one to pass on sympathy, would tell her family she fell off the balcony while painting. Even more later than that she would tell me she basically jumped.

CHAPTER 6
I Love You, Drugs, and Alcohol (But Not Necessarily in that Order)

A couple days after the G incident, Hades randomly called me (I would later find out she was having a day dedicated to GHB). She was at her FFPRMF's place where they were "G'ing out." At some point she decided to call me and tell me how much she was falling for me. Basically she was looking forward to falling in love with me. Of course later on she told me that on G she could fall in love with a totem pole.

After saying, "I want to be the person that loves you," my response was simple but to the point, "Prove it." If she was up for the task, it seemed like an easy thing to do. She then told me she'd be coming over soon. But being, "5 minutes away" isn't quite the same as, "I'll be over in 5 minutes." A few more calls over the next few hours should have showed me just how up to the task she was, however, it was still early in to this and Hades was fun and made me laugh, so the calls were, if nothing else, entertaining.

Then they became serious. She told me that if we were going to move forward, she needed to have a talk with me. That future talk aside, she also said she thought she might be pregnant. My initial reaction was, "Okay, come over and we'll get a test and figure it out." According to her I wasn't reacting enough. It was about at this point that Hades disappeared for a few hours, most likely continuing to "G out."

When Hades finally did make it to my place, she sat me down and this is where the ploy began. She said that if we were going to be together that she needed to tell me everything up front. She told me she had a habit of self-sabotaging herself and her relationships, therefore having this talk was necessary.

This is when she told me about her addiction to GHB and how she self-medicated with Adderall. She had alcoholic tendencies and at times would plan strategic break-ups so she could sleep with someone she was interested in on the side. She was a former coke addict, but went through rehab for that. She knew she would eventually have to go to rehab again, but wasn't ready to stop doing what she was doing.

And for some reason, I accepted her for her faults and all. Most people see red flags as danger, but I, at least at this moment in my life, saw them as challenges. They were laid out like a slalom and if I could ski around each one successfully, at the finish line waited an Olympic Gold medal. Unfortunately, something I didn't realize then is: I can't ski.

I had one rule... well, two really. The first and most important was that she couldn't cheat on me. The other was just communicate and tell me when she was using, for no other reason that I knew what to expect. With that was a request that if she was going to continue using the date rape drug for recreational purposes, she should do so in front of me or with just her FFPRMF, that way she would never be taken advantage of. She agreed and on that we cracked open that pregnancy test... As I suspected it, it was negative.

Hindsight really is 20/20. What I learned from her and looking back on this relationship in its entirety is that to Hades, a little bit of truth is her offense mechanism. She gives you a little bit and tells you it's everything, when in reality there's a whole spectrum of things to find out later. Right out of the box, she told me she was an addict, but a year later she described herself as a poly-addict (someone that is addicted to any and pretty much every substance). Clinically addictive or not, if it entered her, she pretty much needed to keep doing it. In fact, I think she even became addicted to me at one point, but for her current lifestyle, I was probably the most healthy addiction she ever had.

Like everything else in her life, when being "honest," she gives as little as possible and then pats herself on the back for it. She is a human iceberg, revealing 2% of her mass, and hidden beneath the surface is the other 98% of her problems ready to sink unsinkable ships and kill thousands of people in her wake.

To put it best, I borrow a line from Titanic, "This ship can and will sink." And sink I did.

CHAPTER 7
A Different Kind of Courtship

The remnants of her DUI from the previous year lingered on as did a couple guys that Hades had been seeing before we met. There was the hairdresser with the horrible name who wanted to take her out on a fishing boat to gut fish and then the photographer that emailed her a list of 61 reasons why they should be together. She called both of them losers that she somehow ended up with for one reason or another. She constantly thanked me for saving her from being in those relationships.

One thing that was still left from her DUI incident was the matter of community service. She was supposed to fulfill somewhere around the number of 120 hours, but to that day, she had done zero. Mostly because she could never get up early enough to make it down to serve her time. Since she failed to do any of her service and then decided it was best to not check in with the court, she had a wonderful bench warrant out for her arrest.

This was one of the first, but by far not the last things I tried to fix in her life. One night, about a month into our relationship, I was sitting at home and thought Hades would be on her way over soon. At around 10pm, I received a text: totaled my car. Nothing more, nothing less. Several attempts to call her went straight to voice mail. I pictured Hades either injured or standing on the side of the road in handcuffs. As you can imagine, neither image was pleasing.

Hades somehow managed to escape a cell that night even though she had GHB on her. Soon after I had to force her down to the courthouse to deal with her warrant. I remember it was a Friday and she told me it was best to get there early, like 8am early. However on that particular day, like any other particular day, Hades didn't want to get out of bed. It was around noon before she finally woke up. By then, I had showered and put on slacks and a tie... since it was court we were going to. Hades, however, if I remember correctly, wore her Rolling Stones jacket over a T-shirt.

Here's the thing about the whole DUI/Community Service/Getting an extension thing... it sucks. It sucks bad. There's a reason for that too, but hopefully it's pretty self-explanatory. Imagine going to the DMV trying to get a Welfare check. You have to stand in lines just to be told where the next line is. There's two lines for the exact same purpose, but if you get in the wrong one, on the wrong day, they make you go to the other one for no reason whatsoever. Like I said, it sucks.

While standing in one of the many, many lines Hades goes and sits down in the row of chairs across the room. I stood there like a good boyfriend should. At one point she came up and said, "You're the third guy to stand in this line with me." I have to point out a bit of advice to you all... that is NOT the way to win someone over. I'm sure number 1 of 61 reason guy's list was: I POSTED YOUR DUI BAIL.

At the end of the day, she finally stood before the Judge and asked for an extension. It was granted to her and her warrant was dismissed. I was then probably the third guy that was lucky enough to drive her home from court in rush hour traffic. However, I bet I was the first that had to go all the way back when she realized she left her driver's license in the courtroom.

CHAPTER 8
Bless This Mess

When we first started dating and up until the car accident, Hades banned me from coming to her place. You see, whenever she was supposed to come over, I, like a normal person, would clean and straighten up my modest studio apartment. I always lit candles for her and made the mood as nice and as romantic as possible. One of the first times at my place she told me how "calming" it was. My aim was to please and clearly I was doing a good job.

She said I was not allowed to come to her place until she could take the week needed to clean it. How bad could it possibly be? Honestly, I have never met someone as messy as Hades. After her accident, I had to come over so I could drive her back to my place. While making my way up the 101, she texted me, "My place is a mess. We can roll around in the filth."

Now, let's be fair here, I grew up messy (a trait my mom wanted to kill me for) and have spent a lot of my life making paper piles that I will deal with later. But just before Hades and I started hanging out full time, I had an epiphany and one day just straightened up my act. I went through all my closets and threw away anything and everything I didn't need and finally had a spotless place. It's hard to stay as clean as I'd like to be, but I'm working to find the minimalist within.

I walked in the door and for the first time I saw her 2-bedroom condo. It looked like ground zero and all that was missing was the sound of car alarms in the distance. I don't even know where to begin. I took a sabbatical on uploading any pictures anywhere because there was always some random mess in the background. What I do remember from that night was:

-The dirty dishes in the sink, which had a bowl of Lucky Charms from at least a month ago. The milk was hard and moldy and that was on top of a pile of other dishes.

-There was a pile of clothes in the dining room she said the cats peed on.

-Her bedroom floor was covered in clothes, empty wine bottles, empty water bottles, and dirty plates.

-The cats' litter box was at least 3 weeks unchanged.

-Her dog had pooped several times by the pee clothes. The feces was still there.

-Her laundry room was piled knee high with dirty laundry which the cats also peed on.

-There wasn't an inch of room on her bathroom counter and one of the two sinks was completely filled with make-up and other junk.

-There was a hole in the shower wall that was covered in duct tape.

I know my brain blocked out a lot of other things that were too horrifying to retain. After this night she spent the next 6 weeks at my place and within a day it too was a disaster. If a 2-bedroom condo couldn't contain this dirty bomb, my place was no match.
I wish I could be more fair, but this is the truth. I imagine her brain must reflect at least a bit of her disorganized life. Out of order and everything somewhere, but impossible to find.

But, in her defense, as messy as my place was with Hades living there, she did add a certain spice and turned a house into a home. One of her most beautiful assets was her Anne Hathaway-like smile. I remember sitting on the couch while her dad was visiting and she smiled at one of his stories, and it lit up the room. It was just weeks later that I moved out. Her smile was something I adored and the reason I would do anything to make her laugh. It might have been dreadful to come home to a place where you had to step over piles and dishes, but to come home to her smiling face more than made up for it... when she wasn't passed out that is.

CHAPTER 9
Tag, You're It!

It was about 6 weeks into dating. I had a wedding to go to in Maui in 4 months and I already invited Hades to go with me. All things considered, Hades and I were getting along very, very well. The chemistry was amazing, we both laughed constantly, and spent every night together.

It was just before Valentine's Day and Hades and I had our first picture taken together. The FFPRMF took the picture with Hades' camera and she let me have copies of the pictures. By this time many of my friends were asking about Hades, so late that night I uploaded the pictures to Facebook and tagged her. The next morning, I went to my office and pulled up the Facebook pictures. Strangely, the tags had been removed. I was now in a curious predicament. Everything was going well, Hades knew I was uploading the pictures, and she approved of how she looked. So, why would the tags come off? Throughout the day I kept asking myself, "Why would she not want me to tag her?"

I had the feeling that Hades, even though 6 weeks into a relationship, was trying to keep her single appearance. There was still the lingerings of the Hairdresser with the Horrible Name and 61 Reasons Guy, but any and every time those names came up, she seemed relieved to no longer be associated with them. Was I being hidden? There were other guys in her life I got strange vibes from, but she always seemed 100% devoted to us. I mean I was at the office, but she was basically living at my place... she was there at the moment, apparently untagging herself.

I let the untags be for the moment and sent her a relationship request. Throughout the day her page had changed, but the pictures remained untagged and the request was unanswered. That night I asked if she was ashamed of me in some way. The question shocked her but was relevant considering the circumstances. She said she didn't like the way her hair looked, but immediately logged on and retagged herself.

When questioned, especially in the beginning, Hades would immediately correct the situation. She didn't accept my relationship request then but soon enough when I brought it to her attention, she, like this time, logged in that minute and from then on it was Facebook public that Hades was in a relationship with me.

Later Hades would tell me that she compartmentalized me because she basically liked to keep her options open. This was something she said her mom taught her to do. The guys in her life (exes, potential boyfriends, one night stands, etc.) always seemed to disappear on her when she had a boyfriend, and just a month and a half into our thing she wasn't ready to let all of them vanish just yet.

CHAPTER 10
Let's Get Laid

The day Hades totaled her car, that morning when we woke up she was pretty sure it would be the last time going to her current job. It was 8am and with a giant gulp of white wine leftover from the night before, she headed off. (30 minutes later I would get a text: Just threw up for real.)

Throughout the day I received a few pretty loving texts. And at some point she changed her Facebook status to read "Hades is smitten..." Eventually, and as expected, I received an IM from her telling me her position was just cut.

Now was her time to leave the corporate world behind and go for something creative that would leave her more fulfilled. An artist she had met a few months ago scheduled a photo shoot with Hades. During the shoot he offered her an internship with him. She was very excited to be working in a more artistic field. After their shoot and since Hades was car-less, Artist Guy dropped her off at my place and she introduced me to him.

As great as the internship was, she was worried about making money. She received a bit of a severance and was eligible for Unemployment, but randomly one night, again when she was supposed to be on her way over to my place, she told me she was going to an interview. This was about 7pm. For the next hour I received cryptic texts telling me how weird this interview was.

The texts eventually stopped and about 10pm she arrived at my place, her eyes vacant; her face pale. She kept telling me how she was offered an assistant job for a guy whose last name she still didn't know, doing a job that she had little clue about what was expected of her. All she said was she could work from home and make a lot of money, but this guy is really, really mean. The look on her face told me a lot and very little at the same time. What just happened? Where was she the last 3 hours? Whatever it was, wherever she went, this was shady and I knew was not something any new boyfriend would approve of. She later turned down the job and really never spoke of this night again, but it wouldn't be the last time No Last Name Guy would pop into her life.

Six months later, she told me in so many words, that No Last Name Guy was some kind of businessman with no actual business. All his meetings happened at hotel restaurants. If you were to catch him at the end of the day and ask him how he was, he would probably express the dissatisfaction with his day with something such as, "Pimpin' ain't easy."

CHAPTER 11
The G Spot

Hades was happy being an intern and when she was happy, I was happy. She was given the opportunity to stay up late, sleep in, and then go to Artist Guy's studio and help him artistically. For now it would work.

For the most part I would figure in driving her over to the studio into my schedule. Sometimes she had to work nights but, I understood creativity and it doesn't always happen 9 to 5, so I gave her leeway with that. One night she went over there and was then to come back to my place.

Next thing I know, Hades ends up at FFPRMF's place. That is never good, especially after midnight. I immediately get bad thoughts and remember what happened there before. She's texting and calling me every 15 minutes then that stops and she's not picking up her phone. Strangely enough, it was raining, which gave me even stronger feelings of deja vu.

I throw on my jacket, hop in the car, and drive the 5 minutes to FFPRMF's place. And I froze. I stood in the rain, 10 feet from the door, for about 45 minutes. I know what's going on on the other side of the door, but what if I'm wrong? I won't just look like an idiot but also like a lunatic. Finally I knock on the door and some strange woman answers.

"FFPRMF isn't here," she immediately says.

"I'm not looking for her. Is Hades here?"

"Who are you?"

"I'm her boyfriend," and on that note she gives me a suspicious up and down look before closing the door. I wait.

As the door creeks back open, "She says she doesn't want to talk to you."

"Fine," and on that I leave. If this is where she'd rather be, then she can stay there for all I cared. I go home and go to bed. It's still less than 2 months in and if this is how it's going to end, then I just had to accept it.

20 minutes later my phone rings. It's Hades. She asks me if I'm mad at her. I tell her if that's what she'd rather be doing, then she can stay there and do that. She asks if I'll come get her. A few minutes later, for reasons I can't explain, I find myself pulling up to the little shanty on Fairfax.

I call her and tell her I'm outside. She slinks out like a sad Beagle: head down, eyes big, looking up at me with such a pathetic look. She says she can't leave without her stuff, I tell her to go in and get it.

She goes back inside and a few moments later comes back out, again empty handed.

"Where's your stuff?" I ask.

"They won't let me leave," she says quietly.

"I'm about to leave, with or without you, so you better decide now what you're going to do."

For the first and probably the last time I see in Hades' eyes a look of fear. For a split-second, and maybe just no more than that, she was actually afraid I was going to leave her... and I was. She can have her G and her H and her B, but I was about to leave.

I walk back in the Shanty with her and see the woman that answered the door earlier and her weird looking boyfriend sitting on the couch, FFPRMF is in the "bedroom." I use quotes here because the place is smaller than a studio and barely offered a kitchenette, but did somehow separate a bed from the "living room."

We gather her things in silence, FFPRMF sort of looking at me wondering why I'm taking her friend from her. We grab her laptop, backpack, and phone and walk out the door.

"I'm sorry," she says as I start my car.

"I just don't understand what happened."

"I just came to pick something up and they offered me some G."

"I thought we had a deal."

"I know... and I'm sorry."

We drove back to my place and she apologized over and over, just like the first time, and much like the first time I expected her to just pass out when we got there. She didn't. Somehow, Hades learned just how much GHB to take to give her that 20-minute fix and then return her to normal. I wonder just how much of it you have to do to figure out the-feel-good-but-not-too-good-that-you-get-raped formula.

Hades promised this was the last time and said she would make it up to me the next day. She was good at apologies, especially in the beginning.

Hades knew she did a lot of bad things, and the worst moments of her life weren't doing the bad things, but the getting caught doing the bad things. She didn't like to be abandoned, but strangely did a lot crap to make people do just that. It was a sad dichotomy, fear of abandonment yet making it so pretty much everyone that loved you, left you. So she kept doing the stuff that made people leave and people left and she justified in her head that people are going to leave anyway, so why stop doing the things that you do. A continues cycle of saying, "Everyone leaves me anyway, why should I change?"

CHAPTER 12
Nice Ink

One day while I was at work and I believe Hades was at my place watching STEP UP 2: THE STREETS, she called me up and told me she found a job. She sounded very happy with herself as she should be, she was going to re-enter the working world.

I asked what the job was and she said a friend of her's from up North was opening a tattoo parlor in Los Angeles and he wanted her to manage it. Not exactly what I was hoping for, but it was work and she sounded excited about it. That day he was coming down to show her the place he wanted to buy. That seemed fair enough.

That day turned into that evening and I suppose he picked her up around 4, which wasn't too bad, but from my place to Venice and back, meant she wouldn't be back for at least 3-4 hours. This was some kind of old friend of her's and after the parlor tour he ended up taking her out to dinner.

He eventually dropped her off close to 10pm and she came up to my place. She said dinner was with Tattoo Friend and the guy selling the shop in Venice, but she mentioned that at dinner there was little talk of actually buying or taking about the parlor, just buddy buddy talk.

Later that night she received a text and her face dropped. She showed me the text which said, "what if I tried to kiss u?" Well, there went that job and her high hopes of employment. She was devastated and I really felt for her. She had a few drinks to calm herself down and eventually we both fell asleep.

The next morning, as was the routine for every morning, I got up, showered and went to work. But before I left for the office, I tucked Hades in, hunted for her phone and plugged it into the charger. The difference this time was her blackberry was frozen, the screen stuck on a half written email to Tattoo Guy. Basically instead of telling him off for wasting her time, she wrote back something like "I would be lying if I didn't tell you I felt the same way..." If I remember correctly the next sentence talked about how Tattoo Guy and her Ex were friends and how that would look, but she didn't finish before eventually falling asleep.

This should have been enough, but again Hades was really good at telling me she loved me, and I ate that up. She was pretty, made laugh, and we were basically living together here, so what exactly did that text mean? I'm stupid for even digging deeper than what it obviously meant.

That night we were watching THE MACHINIST and I knew I had to bring this up. Eventually she looked at me and asked what was wrong. I told her what I saw. Immediately she stood up, went in the bathroom, and closed the door. She sat in there, alone, for a good 20 minutes. I couldn't tell if she was mad, upset, hurt, or ashamed.

Eventually she came out and said she had to go home. I didn't understand why because we hadn't even talked about it. Running away was not going to make either of us feel better. She accused me of going through her phone and invading her privacy, she eventually changed her tune and said she was drunk and never sent the text, and ultimately sorry for hurting me.

I came to terms and made up the excuse in my head that she was starting to get desperate to make money and although it seemed like the tattoo parlor was just a rouse, if it wasn't, she at least thought she'd be a shoe in for the job.

What this started was an constant wonder what was going on in her phone. Hades spent a lot of time on her phone, but not talking, just texting. Many days and many nights I spent good amounts of time thinking about other texts she could be writing to people like the Hairdresser with the Horrible Name or 61 Reasons Guy. What life could be living inside the virtual world of her cell phone?

I never knew if she did or didn't send that text or what exactly Tattoo Guy thought was going on, either between him and her or her and me. He did pop up from time-to-time and now was another satellite circling planet Hades. This girl had an asteroid belt that competed with Saturn.

CHAPTER 13
Adderall and All for One

Kudos to the doctor/scientist that came up with the brand name for the ADD medication. I always thought it was a clever use of the "ADD"

Hades liked to stay up late and enjoying the playfulness attitude she achieved in the twilight hours of the morning, I ended up staying up with her. The difference between our two lives however was I still had to get to work in the morning, whereas Hades could be 30 minutes late to anything she had planned the next afternoon. There were many nights a week that I was surviving on an hour or two of sleep.

I lived five minutes from my office so I typically would run home for lunch. I would wake Hades up, make her lunch, and spend an hour in the middle of the day with her. It was a nice break in the day and if I didn't wake her up, she might be asleep all day.

On one particular Friday, Hades came to the office with me and worked on some of her internship stuff. After work we went home and talked about watching a movie. We laid down on the floor and ended up dozing off. I don't know how long we were out, but next thing I know I'm waking up to the image of Hades, her stuff in her hands, backpack on her back, heading out the front door. Since I was out cold, she decided she wanted to go spend time with her FFPRMF. It felt like an odd decision, but she swore no GHB would be involved this time. So, with a little feeling of abandonment, I was okay with her going.

Throughout the night, my phone would ring, Hades on the other end asking random questions, "Where were you born?" "What time were you born?" "AM or PM?" She told me she was doing a very intensive, very detailed astrology/relationship chart on us. By the time it reached about 4am, I asked her how we were supposed to spend any of Saturday together if she was going to be up all night. She told me she'd be back soon.

7am rolled around and she finally was done with our star chart and came home. I was, for lack of a better word, disappointed by Hades. I worked all week and the weekends were a time for us to really spend time together. Now I expected her to crash and let me spend the first of two days off alone. That's when she told me how Adderall worked. She pulled out a peach colored pill and broke off a small piece and downed it. When it kicked in, it would allow her to stay up all day. Apparently, on Adderall, Hades needed no sleep.

I will give her that, she did work the Adderall to the best she could and was awake until we both crashed later that night. I may be able to survive on a couple hours of sleep here and there, but I was a big proponent of getting rest. The idea of Hades completely foregoing any sleep really put a pit in my stomach. Zero sleep, as everyone should know, is not a way to survive and it did bother me when she would pull out the peach chip and "Viola" and it was now time to rock the day.

One night we were at dinner and the subject of Adderall came up. Hades told me she, many times over, wanted to just give me her supply so she couldn't self-medicate so easily. I said that was her decision but one I would welcome. She looked at me for a bit, then went into her purse. She pulled out a small Bedazzled case and handed it over. Inside were three peach colored tablets. Now peach is the strongest dose of Adderall and what was originally just a tiny piece, Hades was at this point up to a quarter needed at a time to allow her to stay up two days straight.

We came to a deal and that was I would hold onto it. I wouldn't throw it away and would make it available to her if she asked. She hoped that having to ask me for it would add an extra and somewhat embarrassing step in her process of self-medicating.
I was happy to oblige her and really wanted to help any way I could ween her off the confetti of medications she was taking.

Hades had the ability to get more but for the mean time I was going to trust that she was going to live up to her part of the bargain. I didn't realize it then, but here is where our roles somewhat altered from being boyfriend/girlfriend and I was morphing into more of a parent role.

CHAPTER 14
Can I Get Some Fries with that Shake?

This is a chapter in my life with Hades I knew I was going to have to write but am very well aware it will be harder than many of the other stories I've told yet thus far. This one has burned mental images which I still think about on a daily basis.

Before I met Hades, she was spending most nights with her FFPRMF. In fact the night we decided via e-mail to go out on our real first date, she was at the shanty editing a music video. But now that we were together, her nights over there had been dwindling down to maybe once a week, maybe even no nights a week. The last thing I wanted to do, however, was ostracize her best friend. To do that would be to garner negative talk from a person that was supportive of me being a part of Hades life.

The night before she went out with FFPRMF and her somewhat/pseudo manager. The manager was an old school music guy and FFPRMF was apparently his latest client, or so I was told. I always do my due diligence, especially industry types and it was hard to find many things that backed up what Hades told me this guy had accomplished. At the very least, she was hoping he could help her find a job; at the most he promised to introduce her brother, who was suffering through some mystery illness, to doctors that might be able to help him. If House were a real doctor at a real hospital, Hades' brother would probably be under his care right now. Sad, but true.

She came home with a bottle she said was G mixed in Saki. She wanted to not only do it, but do it with me. The spotlight shone down on me. This was a moment I eventually expected but wasn't sure how I would react.

I'm a clean guy. The worst up until this point I had done was weed. I had been offered cocaine on previous occasions but have always turned it down. One of my favorite "Hollywood" stories was smoking a joint with an A-list musician and an A-list actress. It was a very Hollywood and very surreal moment for a guy from Tucson, Arizona, but I have always turned down anything harder than that.

She took her sip and trying to be open to new things, I put the bottle to my lips. The taste of the salty GHB mixed with the old saki is a taste that will forever live in my long term memory. By that, I mean it was horrible. Unaware of how much to take, I must have let it touch my lips and stopped not much further from there.

Not long after, Hades began to "G out" and stood in the middle of the room humming to herself. I felt a very mild effect of the "awesomeness" she talked about, but overall it really didn't hit me at all. Watching how it affected her, I can see why she did it. It looked much more enjoyable on her than it felt to me.

This night isn't too eventful but necessary to tell to explain the lead up that was the next day. I came home a bit early to find Hades watching an episode of "Housewives of New York." This was one of her guilty pleasures. Afterwards she was going to clean herself up and we were going to go to the art store. Hades hadn't painted in some time and she owed me a painting, so paints and canvas were on her to buy list.

During the first ad of a commercial break, Hades stood up and I heard her shin hit the edge of my coffee table. She immediately went right back down on the couch and groaned as if playing up the pain. I chuckled but looking over at her, that's when I realized there was much more going on. Hades was having a full blown seizure. I had never witnessed this before but her eyes were rolled back into her head, all her muscles were contracted and her teeth were biting down on her bottom lip. I straddled her on my couch and just tried to shout to her through the episode. While doing this, I called 9-1-1. As I gave my address to the operator, Hades' face turned white. I was given a few instructions but they were all going in one ear and out the other. I was, simply, terrified.

The whole process probably lasted less than a minute, but felt like an eternity. Her body eventually relaxed and her color returned. Her blue-green eyes eventually focused on me again and she looked utterly confused. I explained what happened and she started to cry.

I told her the paramedics were on their way and she kept telling me "No, no, no..." while still in a bit of a daze. While she was still protesting, the fire department arrived. They asked their routine questions while loading her onto a stretcher. I tried to stay in her line of sight so she never felt alone and remember mouthing to her, "It's okay. I love you."

They loaded her in the back of the ambulance, and allowed me to sit shotgun for the 5-minute ride to Cedars-Sinai. They wheeled her in to the ER and there were no rooms available so we had to stay in the hallway.

At one point Hades looked at me and asked, "How did we meet?" All of a sudden her brain was what we called Etch-A-Sketch. Pieces of stories missing as if someone shook them right out of her. At least the memories would return when she was given a few clues or bits of information.

We waited in the ER hallway for hours. Nurses would come get her vitals, they wanted her to pee in a cup, which was something she didn't want to do. Even as the sympathetic doctor came to talk to her, Hades was intent on leaving as soon as she could. The doctor ordered a CT-scan, but Hades wanted to go, even if it meant AMA (Against Medical Advice). She said she had been through this before and she feared losing her driver's license again. She agreed that she'd go to a neurologist if we could leave. She seemed okay and if the doctor said she could go, which she did, then who was I to say she couldn't? Of course, Hades was now calling her "seizure" a "feinting spell."

I called one of my good friends and asked if she'd pick us up. I explained a little of the story to her of what happened, but only a bit at a time. Hades was discharged and we drove back home. By this time, at least 6 hours had passed.

My friend cared about me and therefore cared about Hades. This incident clearly worried her. She dropped us off and I helped Hades into the house. Hades sat on the couch and I was going into the kitchen to get her a water. I stood in the doorway and all of a sudden she looked at me with what I now call the fish look. She stared through me in the most emotionless way. Before I could comprehend what was going on, Hades was full blown in another seizure. I rushed over to her and even though was told not to put anything in her mouth, she had already bit her bottom lip from the first seizure, instinctively I jammed the meaty part of my hand in mouth and let her clamp down. I again tried to talk her through it.

Her face started to turn a color that Crayola calls Pale Blue. Watching a loved one turn color from lack of oxygen is a feeling that's too hard to put into words. If you've been there, you know it; if you haven't, then you can't even begin to comprehend just how traumatic that is. All I can say is that it was terrifying. The woman I fell for so quickly, was about to asphyxiate. Her body was still convulsing when I squeezed off her nose and blew two quick breaths into her lungs. I don't know if it was the shock of the sudden oxygen or the force of the blows, but the seizure stopped and immediately the pink color returned to her cheeks.

My friend was already en route back to me as I sent her a message during the episode. Hades again came to and I explained she had another. Again, she wept. She sat up on the couch as I let my friend in my apartment. We stood over her like concerned parents, her confused in post-seizure mode. Finally Hades agreed to go back to the hospital.

I packed a few things in case she would need to be admitted and we checked back in. They took her back and a new doctor was attending her case. This doctor had seen Hades before. I'm not clear if it was for a previous seizure, which she told me about, or something else, but he had little patience with her. This time they got her urine and she admitted to the GHB the night before. As we were in a room this time, Hades turned to me and said, "There's more." I didn't understand what she meant until she continued, "I snorted two lines of Speed last night." She agreed to tell the doctor, who I brought back into her room. She repeated what she just told me and his curt response was nothing more than, "That'll do it." He clearly was much further along with how to deal with Hades than I was.

She apologized. I told her I can't do this again. I can't sit in an ER because of drugs and think about how she almost died in my living room, in my arms. How I had to put life back into her. She nodded and said the Speed was not a normal part of her drug regime, just something that was offered to her out of the blue the night before. She couldn't even give me a good or honest answer, but not even 3 months into our relationship, I accepted it for what it was.

I had no intention of leaving Hades, but knew that she needed some kind of help, maybe help I was unable to offer. I would try and reach out a hand, if she was willing to accept.

Although the ER doctor said it was definitely the Speed, Hades would later give her own diagnosis. Apparently the GHB she, and to some extent, I took the night before was not really GHB. FFPRMF called her later to say there were other seizures happening from that batch of GHB, and what it really was, I don't remember what she called it, but was a form of gasoline.

CHAPTER 15
I'll Take "The Rapists" for One Hundred, Alex

Seizure passed, but what a night it was. I finally brought Hades to my place where I put her into bed and let her pass out. She pretty much slept for the next 24 hours straight. I laid in bed wide awake for hours and kept putting my hand in front of her nose, making sure the slight tickle of air ran over my fingers as she exhaled. She continued to breath into the night. The worst, for now, was over.

I don't remember how many hours or days the Langoliers ate before Hades was considered "missing" by her friends and family. Her phone, usually a constant bustle of action, went unattended as she slept. I could barely walk the dogs (we each had one) without worrying she would seize, stop breathing, and die all in the few moments it took for a Jack Russell mix and a Beagle to do their business. You see, the seizures may have attacked Hades, but, good news for her, she didn't even remember them. Bad news for me is that I did. These memories still etched in my head.

For better or worse it was time to try and help Hades out of her recreational rut, the 5 foot, 6 inch hole she had dug herself into. My reach would only go so far, and six more inches down and she would cross that great divide into a proverbial no-fly zone.

Her roommate befriended me on FaceBook so he could ask me if Hades was with me. My reply was simple and to the point. No need to get into specifics with anyone just yet. She did call her parents from the gurney to tell them what happened. No mention of the drugs (or gasoline for that matter). Knowing her history, they did ask. She denied.

Eventually I emailed my therapist and asked for a duo session. I ran down what happened, typing with my left hand on my blackberry, my right arm wrapped tightly around the sleeping Hades. The LCD the only thing visible in the darkened room, I feared Hades would awake and either see my plan or as the video games I grew up on warned, the startling flash of light might toss her into another seizure.

My therapist agreed to see us. The night before the planned appointment, about day 3 of our isolated time in my place as she recovered fully, I told her I made us an appointment and asked if she'd go. She quietly agreed.

I explained why this was a threesome session and Hades opened up, if only a bit. She explained that at some point, as I explained in an earlier chapter, I became more of a parent figure. That was a fact and I agreed. I didn't want to raise Hades, but seeing her lifestyle and now the dangers of it, I also had a hard time just saying "do all that you did before we met." Her boyfriends of past typically were not good for her and I wasn't one that would be just another drug fueled relationship.

Overall, the session was good, or at least I thought. We walked out of the office a bit silent and had lunch at a place down the street. We talked more and she thanked me for taking her. Was progress made? Perhaps, I didn't expect her to change her habits overnight, but maybe, just maybe she was looking at the fork in the road and maybe she was being drawn to the well lit path for once.

Months later she would tell me that I tricked her into that therapy session. That I never said we were both going to go in. She explained that she thought she was going only because I didn't want to leave her alone and expected to sit in the waiting room during my session.

CHAPTER 16
My Sink Won't Sleep For Weeks

Somewhere in the gap between seizure and trick therapy, Hades was fast asleep and I was replaying the conversation in my head in the hospital where Hades agreed that drugs were not for her anymore. I got out of bed, went to my bag, and pulled out the Peach colored Adderall tablets. There were three in all. I went into the bathroom, dropped them in the sink, and washed them down. Twelve Hades' sized doses (or 24 days of awake) dissolved and disappeared. I felt good.

Weeks later, Hades was at my office. She was supposed to go to a concert that night with Wizrobe, her former "partner in crime." Wizrobe was a guy in the music scene who looked like Merlin, Gandolf, or any cliche wizard from any cliche movie about wizards. This was a relationship veiled in a bit of mystery. He clearly was in love with her but Hades denied any feelings whatsoever for him. She told me before that telling him she was in a relationship was going to kill him but he was going to have to back off his unrequited attempts at love.

One night, previous to this event, Hades was to go see Wizrobe and told me she was going to have that talk. Afterward she made her way over to my place and walked in carrying a bass (the instrument, not the fish). I looked at her confused and she said, "The good news is I didn't have to have the talk with him and the better news is he gave me a bass." Odd, it seems a somewhat lavish gift might mean the "talk" was even more necessary, but apparently in the Underworld of Hades, elaborate gifts mean you continue to lead people on until the gifts stop naturally.

Anyway, she fell asleep on the couch in my office while I finished up work. Her phone kept ringing, but she slept through the generic blackberry ringtone. I saw on the screen it was Wizrobe. She ended up canceling that night due to extreme exhaustion. I took her to my place, we ordered dinner, and she feel asleep half way through "YES MAN." She then woke up and strangely asked where her Adderall was. Granted the deal was I would hold on to it, but again, thinking back to our "No More Drugs" hospital conversation, I informed her the Adderall were now gone.

"Idiot," she exclaimed before falling back to sleep. She woke up later and through the next day didn't mention the Adderall trashing again. The next night she received a call from a girlfriend asking if she wanted to bartend a house party in just a few short hours. She agreed.

This is where my insecurities kicked in. At this point we had 61 Reasons Guy, Hairdresser with the Horrible Name, Tattoo Guy, Wizrobe plus a couple others not yet mentioned circling Hades. All I needed was a handful of new guys from the cheesy house-party trying to add themselves to her mix. I told her just that. She really didn't react much to that, other than to say that no guy at some lame house-party was going to woo her from me. Had this been a normal girl and not a harpy, I might have been good with that answer. But, this was Hades and Hell was her game. I drove her home and after a few texts she went radio silent.

It was probably around 3:30am when I woke to my phone ringing. It was a number I didn't recognize. "Hello?" I answered.

"I locked myself out of my phone," Hades said using her roommate's cell. I was more or less just confused. She was complaining about not being able to unlock her blackberry. And after the 10th attempt, just after she called, it reset to factory settings. She just wiped out her contacts, texts, etc. I think she had been drinking.

We then started to argue. I still had her dog and decided to return it and confront her face-to-face. Arguing with Hades on the phone was always a no-win, worst case scenario incident. I hate fighting to begin with but on the phone Hades tended to mumble and our fights became me repeating, "What," "Huh," or "Say again?" more times than I cared for. Therefore if it was a petty fight or worth fixing immediately, I had to get in the same room with her. Sometimes it was exhausting, but usually after 30 minutes of one-on-one time, we would come to terms and enjoy the rest of the day. If we continued by phone, it would go in circles for hours, and then we'd both be mad and not talk to each other for a couple days.

I arrived at her place, both dogs in tow. She was somewhere on that side of intoxicated as she lay on the couch. She was not happy. The resentment she held in the past 24 hours started to come out. She was upset about the Adderall and made it very clear. She schooled me on how addicts work, that even if they aren't using, the opportunity to use is always better than not being able to. It was at this point that she told me she just wanted to "get trashed" on anything she could get her hands on. She canceled Hawaii and said she couldn't bear to look my friends in the face knowing they knew about the seizures.

Eventually around 5am she passed out. I stayed there hoping that when she woke up, she would realize all the things she did and said. When her eyes opened, I was watching FORGETTING SARAH MARSHALL, a movie we watched a dozen times. It had a great effect of making us forget whatever stupid fight was going on. We went out to lunch and made up. Everything was back to normal. However, it was now the Saturday before Easter and you already know how that night went.

CHAPTER 17
Gonna Set My Soul, Gonna Set My Soul On Fire..."

It was a weekend away from our three month anniversary and Hades had to go to Las Vegas for a immediate family reunion of sorts. Her mother was celebrating the fact she was becoming a septuagenarian and decided Las Vegas was the hub of where her sons and daughters should venture. Hades was to be gone for 3 days. After she packed last minute, I drove her to the airport where she was about 5 minutes away from missing her flight. On the way home I called the hotel and had chocolate covered strawberries delivered to her room.

This was the longest time that Hades and I would spend apart since we started seeing one another. I jokingly sent her a text saying I would happily drive the 4 hours for a chance to see her, enjoy a little time in Vegas with her, and meet her family. Surprisingly, Hades took me up on the offer.

The plan was I would drive out the next afternoon. Late that night, after thanking me for the surprise, Hades told me she mentioned the rendezvous to her mother, who she said almost cried as we would be taking the attention off her birthday. Therefore, it became a secret rendezvous, which was actually very exciting to me.

I drove out, booking a room at the Bellagio, where Hades was staying with her family. Upon arrival, I texted her. Within minutes she appeared at my door. It was like we were having an affair on each other. She could only stay a moment as she told her family she was getting something from the room and it was back down to dinner. I told her I was going to sit at the adjacent bar and get a voyeuristic feel of her family. The idea excited her.

The bar was across the restaurant and I sat at the end just a bit out of sight. Hades came over on the way to the bathroom and we did a shot together. She had to get back to dinner and then attend the Cirque show, but afterward the night was ours.

She appeared back in my room where I had a chilled bottle of vodka waiting. We downed a few shots and then hit the Strip. We landed in Paris for a bit of roulette, watched the fountain at Bellagio and eventually had a very, very early breakfast in the Planet Hollywood Cafe.

We finally made it back to my room and she stayed as late as she could, about 11am the next morning. She told me she told her sisters I was there, but other than that, my visit to Vegas still was hush hush.

She departed and I hung out a bit in Sin City prepared to stay another night if another affair was possible. She was supposed to hang with her family and then for her 70th, her mother, sister and Hades were going to get tattoos. She was going to be tied up, so I drove back home. I was to pick her up from the airport the next day. She had yet to send me her itinerary.

Tattoo guy just happened to have a parlor in Vegas, which meant they saw each other during her visit there as he was doing the family tattoo job. Overall, I didn't feel threatened. I was still in bliss and had yet to know the true sociopathic tendencies of my girlfriend, so I really wasn't all that worried.

The next day I called and texted Hades trying to get her flight info. Hades was MIA as if she disappeared off the face of the planet. Around 5pm she finally reached out with nothing more than a simple, "family fighting, staying another night." I called her and she was able to talk no more than about 20 seconds before cutting me off, telling me she'd call me right back. Hours passed until I received a simple text informing me she couldn't call. I told her to send me her updated flight info and I'd pick her up the next day.

I woke up, it was Monday and still not having the vital info to do the simple act of picking up my girlfriend from the airport, I went to work. I tried calling her, but her phone just rang. Since the phone rang, I assumed she had yet to turn it off for the flight. But around noon she called, telling me she landed but since her phone was "dead" she couldn't call me so she just cabbed it home. This was really curious considering the few times I did try her, the phone rang. Again, today was just our three month anniversary so when things didn't quite make sense, I just blew them off instead of really paying attention to inconsistencies.

I bailed out of work and was at her place by 1pm with flowers. It was good to see her, two days seemed like an eternity to not really see or hear from her.

It was early in our conversation she mentioned that Artist Guy made some flippant comment about her place. Strangely, Artist Guy had never been to her place before. That's when she explained to me that he popped by earlier that day because he happened to be in the area.

This is about when I started to analyze facts, timestamps on texts, and receipts that happened to be laying around the house. Was Hades as committed as she said or was I being played? This question was interrupted by the story of the guy that she happened to sit next to on the plane. This one happened to work in the music industry and offered to help her on a song project she was knee deep in.

Welcome to the party, Lame Music Guy.

CHAPTER 18
That's What I Like About You

We're starting to move into the shady territory here and I need to make a few things clear. Living in the situation is a lot different than looking back on it. Inconsistencies up until now and even further along went either unnoticed or were just too unbelievable to think twice about them. If my head was as clear as it is now, there would have been easier ways to deal with certain situations, but then there'd be no book.

What I'm worried about as I get further into this tale is that you will just think me foolish for 1. Not seeing the tell-tale signs and 2. Staying in this relationship. This is much more than just a "I took the abuse because I loved her" situation. Dealing with a sociopath is far, far worse than anything I could have ever imagined in a relationship. There's a reason Ted Bundy was such a womanizer and there's a reason so many women fell for him. Sociopaths lack empathy and make up for that with charm. Hades was, if nothing else, charming to the Nth degree. Everybody that came in contact with her, wanted more of her. It wasn't just because of her good looks, but just how good she made you feel.

Artist Guy once told Hades that everything she did and said took on a certain sexuality, layered with undertones that made men not just want, but need more. Frankly, I thought that was bullshit. To the naïve, maybe, and I told Hades that. What I felt was, and excuse the lame cliche example, but an onion and on the surface, yes there was beauty and a certain level of sexuality, but underneath it all was so much more. She was both mysterious and guarded, but also open and free-spirited. Her enigmatic persona defied reason and logic, yet made complete sense. Not many people were lucky enough to make it through the first few levels of depth, but as I kept spelunking, there was so much more to her, that it was insulting that Artist Guy (and so many others) felt nothing more than their primal sexual urges. There was a lot more to Hades than sex, and to the core, whatever made her tick, is sometimes frightening to think about.

As we venture into stories that will make you wonder what I was thinking, know that many times, I simply wasn't. I will try to allow you to see and know what I saw and knew at the time, but remember these stories are told after the fact, months later, with more insight.

Bear with me and please hold your applause until the end. We've got a long way yet to go. Thank you.

CHAPTER 19
I Take Two Steps Forward, You Take Two Steps Back

I'm having a hard time remembering exactly where this story takes place in the grand scheme of things, as I'm sure it's important to know where my head was at the time. I knew I loved Hades and Hades loved me (whatever that word meant to her specifically, I do not know). Besides being a Sociopath, Hades showed classic signs of a Borderline Personality Disorder. Borderlines have a duality to them. They either love you(+) or they hate you(-). There is no middle. This is called Splitting or Idealization and Devaluation.

It's a rather amazing thing to watch and if Borderlines were animals, there'd be tens of hundreds of documentaries on them. Sir Richard Attenborough's voice would narrate as a cameraman would lie in waiting on some African plain. The Borderline would show complete devotion to another, then like flipping a switch, she takes a defensive stance, rears on her hind legs, and shows her eye spots ready to rip out her loved one's throat. For some reason, reminds me of the Praying Mantis.

There will be a few of these stories. The first was one night she was working for Artist Guy at one of his shows. She wanted to invite me but insisted that being the lowly intern she was not allowed to invite anyone. We texted back and forth through the evening and into the wee hours of the night. Finally close to 4am, she informed me, via text, she was drunk downtown and wouldn't be coming back to my place. I was upset, not just at the fact that she was "drunk" and somewhere "downtown" but that I waited up while the show not only ended, but she was somehow now downtown when the event was in Hollywood. That started our first fight, but this story is about the next time I was the witness to the splitting.

About a month before what I'm about to get into, Hades had a broken computer that was covered under warranty. Luckily, the warranty included a loaner computer. One night, at Hades' place, her Wacked-Out Neighbor came over. He did this randomly from time-to-time to invade our space and flaunt his odd behavior. Whacked-Out Neighbor was some kind of addict and was always asking Hades for Adderalls or anything else he was looking for that particular night. Frankly he was a bad influence and his random visits were a bit on the creepy side. However, he had recently lost two family members so Hades, trying to relate to him, attempted to welcome his odd behavior since "she had been there."

Hades' home, as you know, was a disaster. One of the most annoying things was she literally owned about 3 drinking glasses and they were always dirty. I ended up using a martini glass one night since it was the only thing clean. About 20 seconds later, I accidentally knocked over the glass, which spilled... all over the borrowed laptop. Internally some things were shot. The mousepad and keyboard were no longer functioning and booting it up took about 5 minutes.

More drastic however was the internal Hades switch was flipped. She went to her room and shut the door and shut down. She hated me and although I apologized, showed her ultimately the computer worked, and offered to pay to replace it, she asked me, at 5am, to leave.

The next day I received texts about how the computer was destroyed and all the work she had done for Artist Guy was lost. Her internship was at risk. I felt horrible. After a full day of regretting the simple act of spilling water, I met her at Fry's. She refused to acknowledge or talk to me, but at the end of the day, I bought the MacBook. That spill cost me $1600.

It was my fault and I was fine with paying for it, but the anger and silent treatment were completely uncalled for. All night I received texts how she fucked up and how angry Artist Guy was at her. She was destined to lose this internship because I screwed up.

After a few days she calmed down. The anger subsided and she was back to her polar opposite of loving me.

After I realized how Hades worked her black magic, I figured out she picked fights for no other reason but to gain control as well give herself a little time to make sure others were still interested.

Artist Guy was never mad at her, in reality he had a thing for her and all those texts that night were complete lies. The files she lost never existed and the moment she "loved" me again, she never mentioned it. The MacBook itself may take a few extra minutes to boot up, but with a keyboard and wireless mouse plugged in, works just as good as before.

I'm using it now to write this book.

CHAPTER 20
A Thug is a Thug is a Thug

Hades and I had planned on spending this particular night together, but she had to go to dinner with FFPRMF's "Manager" first. This was one of those situations where things didn't feel right, but the guy must have been 65 if he was a day. I convinced myself he has to be harmless, besides Hades told me he knew all about me, and said he even asked about me from time-to-time. She was hoping he'd help her find a job, but doing my due diligence, he seemed to have much less power than Hades seemed to think he had. In fact, none of my music industry friends had any idea who the "Old Dude" was.

After her dinner I came over and found that Whacked Out Neighbor decided he was moving out of his mom's place and was using Hades' condo as a storage unit. Everything he owned was in the middle of her living room, in her hall closet, and her bedroom. It wasn't just odd, but very rude. Whacked Out Neighbor had little regard for boundaries. For example, one time when Hades was moments away from tears because she was so far into overdraft, Whacked Out

Neighbor kept asking if she had quarters so he could go do his laundry.

Then around 3am, while Whacked Out Neighbor was getting ready to crash, Hades received a call from Joey the Thug. Joey the Thug is the one and only name I am not changing, because the scum doesn't deserve the respect. Joey the Thug was driving by and noticed the lights were on, so he decided to take it upon himself to pop on over... at 3am.

He walked in and "thug" barely begins to describe this guy. Apparently this guy was in an on-again, off-again relationship with another of Hades' friends, Once Famous Video Vixen, but right now they were off-again. Joey the Thug sits his thug ass down and acts like... yup, a thug. Hades for some reason is acting like they are best friends and later asked me why I wasn't being accommodating to her "friend." I explained to her, as best I could, that Joey the Thug was a thug and had no reason to be over at 3am. She didn't seem to see it my way.

I hovered over Hades trying to figure out thug's angle. I eventually fell asleep on the couch and when I woke up at 7am, Hades and Joey the Thug were gone. I walked around the building, unable to find them. Whacked Out Neighbor at least felt the same as I did: Joey the Thug was no good.

When I woke up, I found Hades phone laying on the floor, which was strange since she never let disappear from her side. I used it to call Joey and within minutes Hades and the Thug returned. She said they were talking in the club house down the hall.

This is when any normal person would leave, but Joey the Thug was not normal. Hades and I disappeared to talk (i.e. argue) about Joey's intentions. The main question being, "Why was he still here?" Joey the Thug basically was waiting for me to leave so he could make his move. Hades was supposed to go to the dog park with Whacked Out Neighbor's mom that morning, which she did. I, as her boyfriend, joined. Joey the Thug, as her thug, joined us as well. Hades and I drove together fighting the whole way there, Thug took his own car. Afterward, he came back to her place and, as thugs do, sat there like a fucking thug.

This is when I told Hades about the strange and anonymous email I received two days before. In so many words, an anonymous emailer told me to be careful because Hades was a cheater.

After Joey the Thug finally left, Hades and I called a truce. She had to attend her court ordered MADD class that night but I thought it would be nice to escape for the weekend and go up to Ventura. She agreed. All in, it was a pretty nice ending to a shitty day.

Ever since the Tattoo Guy text, I always wondered what kind of secret life was being lived within the world of Hades' phone. I didn't need an anonymous email to tell me shit was going on. In my life I have never invaded anyone's virtual privacy and I had no intention of starting now. But for 30 minutes that morning, I read every text on Hades' phone.

CHAPTER 21
In Memoriam...

Strangely enough, I'm writing this chapter on the one year anniversary of the weekend it all unfolded. It was just before Memorial Day weekend when I looked through Hades' phone. We had our Hawaii trip earlier in the month, which was amazing. Every one of the seven days we discussed the possibility of staying there. If it were financially doable, we might still be there, living a different life, in a different time.

I looked through her phone... and for some reason, after seeing the texts, I invited Hades to Ventura. A getaway for all getaways, I suppose.

All I knew at this moment was that I did not exist. As I presumed, not many in Hades' Underworld knew about me. I didn't need Clarance to show me Hades' life if I had never been born, it was all here in 160 characters or less. Hades was definitely with me, but she was playing every single guy in her life: Tattoo Guy, Lame Music

Guy, Artist Guy, Wizrobe, etc. They were all there, being led on, in their own ways. Lame Music Guy mentioned something about going back to Moon Shadows (a restaurant/bar in Malibu) with her. The original outing was never mentioned to me before. Tattoo Guy hadn't stopped his attempts to court his once friend's girlfriend. Artist Guy asked if he could pick her up from the airport when she returned from Hawaii... he seemed to think she was on the islands alone. She said it wasn't necessary, but didn't say it was her boyfriend giving her a ride, but her Best Guy Friend.

The saddest part was Hades didn't just react, but sent out her own random "miss u" texts like distress signals from a sinking ship, too lonely to accept its fate. I sat there, in Hades' living room, post sunrise in a numb and quiet revelation. My blindfold had been lifted, and what was seen could not be unseen. Was I a powerless Captain destined to go down with this ship?

I was so in shock I didn't even know how to react and waiting for Joey the Thug to leave didn't help the situation. How could this be? She says she loves me. How can this be? She once told me she didn't know how to be normal without me. How should this end?

Hades left to attend her MADD class for her DUI sentence, part of me didn't think she was really headed there, but maybe that too was a lie and she was off to meet up with some guy. I no longer thought clearly. How much did I not see? What more did I miss?

That day I went home in tears. She called me that afternoon to tell me just how much I meant to her. We had talked about moving in together and tomorrow before we drove North, she wanted to look at some apartments. I agreed knowing that we would never live under the same roof. How could we? Especially now?

I became a shell of my former self. I tried to figure out a way to break it off. A part of me was now missing and emotionally cut-off. Yet, I still loved her. She was to come over later that night and I planned for us to part ways. Being a writer, I wrote out everything I was supposed to say. I even bought her a parting gift, a way to help me say good-bye.

We did look at apartments, my emotionless self asking about square footage and deposits in homes I knew I would never live. We did drive up to Ventura, a trip I didn't think we would make. I even waited to the last minute to make the reservation. Upon the initial idea of going up there, I had a horrible plan to dump her 100 miles from home, leaving her there to find her own way back. We took her car, which meant that ultimately wasn't a possibility.

One night in Ventura, turned into two. We talked about us, what I knew hadn't come up. It was Sunday morning when I finally told her what I did; what I saw. She immediately turned into the emotional zombie I had been for the last three days. We both shut down. What to say, what to do? The future of living in a Hawaiian village was now a dark highway. Was it salvageable?

She admitted to everything. How could she not? I saw it all. At that moment she probably wished she really lived in that world she created where she was single and I didn't exist. She denied cheating on me and I wanted to believe, if that, nothing else. As an addict, she wasn't just a user of substances, but also people. She said she needed the attention from guys or else she didn't feel worthy of being human.

We agreed to stay another night, if just to discuss and decide where things were going to go. I felt myself weakening. We needed to talk but also needed time apart. I drove back to Los Angeles, her home specifically, to feed her cats. It would be about 3 hours before I returned. We both just sat there, staring off into the void. I was betrayed, she said she felt the same.

We talked over dinner. I told her I wanted to work it out if she wanted the same but only if she was capable of not seeking attention from others. She said she could and in return I wouldn't go through her phone again. All this said, everything on the table, my trust was a raw and open wound. It was up to her to prove herself and let it heal, scarred maybe but stronger, or else the exposed nerve would eventually just lose any capacity left to feel.

Happy Memorial Day.

CHAPTER 22

... --- ...

The date was May 27th, it was two days after our return from Ventura, 72 hours from our talk and revelations about secret friends, texts, and quite possibly relationships. The trust between us was, for lack of a better word, gone. I wondered for some time what was going on behind my back, and now that I knew, I couldn't help but completely become not just overwhelmed but obsessed with what Hades was doing when not in my line of sight.

This particular evening, Hades had to meet up with Lame Music Guy, someone she immediately told me after meeting him that he knew all about me and that she was in a relationship. She also seemed to have meetings with him that I wasn't told about. I should have walked away, or as someone recently said, "peaced out." Easier said than done.

It was too late, I was now heading down a sick road of constantly needing reassurance that Hades either was or wasn't being faithful. If she wasn't, I needed some kind of actual proof beyond the texts. I wanted smoking gun proof, otherwise I would find some way to explain away her behavior. I think I was starting to become even sicker than she. It's one thing to do this stuff to someone else, it's another to let someone do it to you.

Hades and Lame Music Guy were supposed to meet up for dinner, then go see a band together. I was not invited as it was "business" and because they were going to meet up with Wizrobe later. Wizrobe was infatuated by Hades. He also happened to be the son of a doctor who was looking over Hades' brother's medical records. She had to avoid "upsetting" Wizrobe's jealous nature or else he would retract his father's help in trying to pinpoint the brother's mysterious and possibly fatal condition. All in all she was most likely using her brother's illness to keep me out of certain parts of her life that she still needed/wanted to appear single.

Hades obviously knew that our relationship was on the rocks and her faithfulness was under scrutiny. She told me a few times that evening that she loved me and that I had nothing to worry about because, "we were on a new beginning of complete honesty." I hoped for the best, feared the worst. She was either going to do her best to not just change, but mend her ways, or she was going to look me in the eye and lie to my face.

I was awake most of the night and even ended up driving around at 2am to clear my head of the thoughts I had about Hades. It wasn't until 4am that she called me to tell me she got home okay. She was clearly drunk and started rambling about how much she hated guys. Apparently Wizrobe and his friends made fun of her which turned into how she thought all guys wanted her just for sex and nothing else. She even accused me of that. She was drunk, so I let it go. Slowly her ramblings shifted into that of an exhausted mumbling.

I was ready to let sleep but then she said, "I fucked up tonight." I was silent. She didn't see one but two of the guys she was leading on that night and she didn't get home until 4am, so what exactly did she do? She wouldn't elaborate. She said she would tell me more when she saw me the next day.

I couldn't sleep after her ill-timed confession. I was to take her to court the next day. I made my way to her place at noon, as planned, and was ready to be heartbroken from whatever it was she did that justified saying that she "fucked up."

I rolled up to her place and buzzed the door. Her roommate let me in and said Hades was still asleep. Hades wasn't just sleeping but hungover. She was in no shape to appear before a judge. Luckily we had a couple more days before another bench warrant would be issued.

I hung around for a couple hours as she lethargically rose from the undead world of drinking. I noticed she was dressed in her pink Victoria's Secret nightie, which she said she liked to wear because it was comfortable. I asked her what happened the night before and how she "fucked up." She said she didn't remember saying that and although wearing lingerie, nothing out of the ordinary happened.

Part of my driving around that night just so happened to cruise by her place, where I saw her parked in Lame Music Guy's car for an extended amount of time. I wasn't able to see in the windows, but did watch as she went inside by herself. I don't know what exactly happened in the car. Hades told me that he tried to kiss her, but she refused his advances. Did she? Who really knows? I do know that Lame Music Guy soon disappeared for good.

I was about to devote myself to figuring out the level of Hades honesty or distrust. I drew a line in the sand and stared at it. On this side was a healthy version of myself, who had respect for himself and wouldn't stand for this type of infidelity. On the other, was the unhealthy version of me that was going to go to every dark place of his mind to try and salvage something that never was. As I looked down again at that line, I noticed something strange... it was already behind me.

CHAPTER 23
How Are Ya? How Are Ya? How Are Ya?

It feels a bit unfair to post all the bad stuff. It doesn't just make Hades look shrill, evil, and bad to the core, but also makes me look like some kind of fool. Therefore, let's take a moment to reminisce about some of the good.

The trip to Maui was fantastic. We were there to attend one of my best friend's weddings, her dream ceremony. It was beautiful. However, it was this trip that I inadvertently started choosing Hades over friends, friends I had for many years.

The trip started out like any trip with Hades: Late. We already went shopping. Hades wasn't in a good place financially to be taking a trip such as this. I had already paid for the flight and the hotel room was covered mostly in hotel points, but Hades and I needed a small shopping trip to be covered in the attire department. I knew she would balk at me paying for her new clothes, so I gave her an old gift card that had $50 on it. We didn't have that much to buy, so it seemed like it might be adequate. However, when I noticed the tally topping $100 on her end, while she made her final trip in the dressing room, I snuck off with the clerk and added another $50 to the card. All in she paid roughly $18 for her items.

Hades was horrible at packing. We were about to spend 7 days in Maui and Hades had no idea what she needed. Filling a suitcase was one of Hades phobias. She lamented around avoiding it at all costs. When the trip was over, Hades wore pretty much three different outfits, a bikini, and a dress for the wedding. Packing should have taken roughly an hour. Hades was packing for approximately 8 hours when I came over to help her finish. It took us another 4 hours and we had just enough time to go back to my place, calling a cab on the way to take us to LAX.

Upon arriving at LAX, I put Hades' giant suitcase on the baggage scale and it came in at a whopping 70 pounds. That translated to a $100 weight fee. I paid it so we could get on the plane as soon as possible. I knew once we sat ourselves down on the flight, I could finally relax. As a side note, one of the items Hades packed was a fur-lined coat. Yes, one item you always need in Maui in May is a fur coat. I still don't understand Hades' packing rituals, but once you mention the act to her, her ADD kicks in, takes over, and shuts her down.

Hades was still a pretty new relationship, as we were hitting the four month mark during the trip, I did want to spend all my time with her. That meant that somehow I missed a lot of the wedding activities of my friend. Looking back, I can't believe how bad of a friend I really was during this and much of the rest of the time with Hades.

The seven days were flawless. Hades and I drank by the pool, explored the island, and had an amazing first trip together. We did in fact discuss staying indefinitely. We looked at house brochures and tried to figure out how we could sell her condo in L.A. and live out the rest of our lives in Maui. At the time it just wasn't financially or career smart to do so, but the idea of it lingered, which we talked about many times over the course of our relationship.

The last day in Maui, I knew we'd miss our flight if I left packing up to Hades. Therefore, I sent her to the spa while I tried as hard as I could to fit everything we had sparingly between our bags. It was my goal to get her giant suitcase under 50 pounds to avoid that C-note fee. I guesstimated to the best of my ability... the bag came in at 49.5 pounds all in.

The Hawaii trip was perfect. The memories are still amazing. Hopefully since I made my mental and, at times, physical absence up to my friends. Like I said, when Hades was in it, she was amazing. A beautiful and smart woman that made me laugh constantly.

There was so much I didn't know then and I have to admit that the ignorance was bliss. There are things I should have done differently while on the islands, but at the time, I wouldn't have traded that trip for the world.

CHAPTER 24
The Man, The Myth, The Legend

Joey the Thug was, in the simplest terms, a no good thug. I would like to think that I attempt to find the good in people, but the moment I laid eyes on good ol' Joey, my mind was instantly made up. There was nothing noble in this guy.

If the aura of his *thugocity* wasn't enough, it was quickly that certain things came to light. I learned Joey was a drug dealer. In fact, he was the drug dealer that sold Hades the bad batch of G that was pretty much gasoline. The one thing I do give credit to Hades for was the fact that she blamed only herself for that. It was her addiction that allowed her to ingest that. Joey the Thug just happened to be the guy she paid to allow herself to do it.

Joey was also a two time felon, and was, any day now, going to strike out on California's wonderful three strikes law. Support it or not, this was exactly the guy it was meant to put away. The sooner he took a third swing at the ball, the better. Hades however "saw the

Joey

> You know I like you a lot, don't trip cause I'm not gonna sweat you. When you want to see me you'll call. Just don't keep me waiting too long.

Jul 16, 2009 8:08 PM

> I won't. :) :)

Jul 18, 2009 12:35 AM

> Hey what's up? Sorry kind of hard to talk because im in icar with chris on the way to Vegas. Everything ok?

Jul 18, 2009 12:56 AM

> Wtf. I'm going to vegas too, the monte carlo 22323, I think that's the room everybody s

good in him" and wanted to help turn his life around.

She went out of her way to get her father to write a letter on Joey the Thug's behalf so he could find himself one of those things called a "job." To this day, I have no idea why she would take on this charity case. He wanted to better no one nor himself.

After too long, Hades eventually did stop talking to Joey (or maybe it was the other way around), but thankfully he disappeared into the world he created for himself. Last time I saw Hades she told me I was right about Joey. From her lips to my ear, she told me he finally did strike out and was back in prison. This time for G'ing girls out, and while they were high as kite, he would rape them. He did this without protection and knowing full well that he was HIV positive.

It's called the Date Rape Drug for a reason.

CHAPTER 25
The 61 Reasons

While gathering my things and moving out, I had to go through mountains of papers, cluttered closets, and rooms covered from wall-to-wall. It was quite a task, especially when I had moved in only 4 months before. Well, in my attempt to find everything that was mine, I happened upon a printed email: the 61 reasons email. It isn't just a list, but 7 pages in what must be 6-point font. I still have yet to read the entire thing, or even the full list for that matter.

I debated whether it was in good form to reprint the list here. I suppose I shouldn't really care that much about etiquette as I spent many nights dealing with Hades after she got off the phone with 61 Reasons Guy: the anger, the victim mentality, and having to pump her spirits when 61 would trash her and make her feel bad. I mean as she put it, they didn't even really "date." At the point he sent this, we had been dating a couple months. He even opens with the following: "I wrote this back in September and October before we went our separate ways. Unfortunately during that time, you repeatedly stated you were too sensitive to discuss most of these items, so I never sent the email. During November and December I was still hoping we'd at least get a chance to discuss it as friends, and that opportunity never materialized either. At the time I wrote this, unlike now, I thought things still had a chance to work out, so I was trying to be optimistic, but you can certainly feel free to ignore any of the parts at the bottom where I say I hope things work out and that I still love you, etc. I would go back now (Feb.) and edit that out, but it's accurate to how I felt at the time, so I've left it alone. I considered several times just deleting this entire email altogether, but decided against it, and in the hope that you gain some useful insight into yourself rom how you appeared to me, I figured I'd just go ahead and send it, mostly because I'm tired of it sitting there un-sent, mocking me...and well, maybe it'll make your next breakup go smoother." Overall, 61 Reasons Guy is probably not nearly as bad as I built him up in my head. He made some really valid points. My favorite being, "Sometimes I think you say, 'I love you,' when you really just mean, 'thank you.'"

Unfortunately, she did many of the things to him that she later tried and/or did with me. Since this is an anonymous forum, I present you with the list:

60 [sic] REASONS WHY I AM THE BEST BOYFRIEND YOU'VE EVER HAD!

1. I actually like to cuddle.
2. I have bedroom eyes.
3. I love being a guy.
4. I can hang with you and your girlfriends without hitting on them.
5. I do not wear tighty-whities.
6. I respect women.
7. I stay in shape.

8. I love animals especially ones that taste like chicken. the rest are nice too, as long as I don't breath [*sic*] furballs, that's all.
9. I'll remember our anniversaries.
10. I don't pick my teeth at the table.
11. I listen.
12. I'm genuine.
13. I'll charm your family.
14. I keep my nails trimmed.
15. I'm 5'10" tall, dark, and handsome.
16. I'll massage you if you have a tough day or even an easy one.
17. I like making love as much as wild, sweaty monkey-fucking.
18. I do not have any STDs.
19. I'll take care of you when you're sick.
20. I am well educated.
21. I'll bring you flowers.
22. I'll take baths with you, now that I have two tubs.
23. I'll never ask you to get a boob job.
24. I'm in touch with my own feelings.
25. I put the seat down!
26. I will always be there for you.
27. I will look at you in the eyes when we talk.
28. I communicate.
29. I don't think farting is a sport.
30. I want a happy joyous future.
31. I'm not obsessed with watching sports.
32. I'm up for spooning anytime.
33. I groom down there.
34. I take out the garbage without being asked.
35. I'm honest.
36. I'm a good athlete in most sports.
37. I'll whisper sweet nothings in your ear.

38. I'll call when I say I will.
39. I'll leave you secret love notes.
40. Given the opportunity, I'll wear your ass as a hat (that's just an expression)
41. I'll plan romantic getaways.
42. I will make you laugh.
43. I'm not into road rage.
44. Did I say I'm honest?
45. I will sweep you off your feet.
46. I have a warm smile.
47. I'm not afraid of commitment.
48. I'll surprise you.
49. I'm strong but gentile [sic].
50. I'm intelligent.
51. If you're having trouble getting up for work, I make it a point to call you every day to help you, even if it shortens my own sleep.
52. Magnum XL
53. I walk into Costco, and the first thing I look for is contact solution and extra tooth brushes. I don't wear contacts and have a spinner brush.
54. I cleaned out my garage so you could park your car.
55. I started shopping for a night table so you'd have a place to put your stuff.
56. I programmed stations you like on my internet radio and on my trucks fm radio.
57. I stock my fridge with things you like to drink and my closet with chicken broth and cereal you like.
58. When we go to the movies, I ask you what you want to sce?
59. When we watch tv I ask you what you want to watch?
60. When we go out to dinner I ask you what kind of food you're hungry for?

61. I'm the guy that wants you to go to MY high school reunion with me. I'm the guy that wants to meet your family and wants you to meet mine. I'm the guy that wants to meet your friends, and you mine.

CHAPTER 26
Highway to Hell

Court date number two was looming and as expected, Hades waited until the very last day to check-in. It was expected because she had yet to fulfill even one hour of her community service. She decided she wanted to use her pseudo diagnosis from the balcony incident as a way to either extend or possibly even get out of the physically demanding act of community service. Her last court visitation assigned her clean-up duty at a golf course. This time, with the CT Scan and a few "nodes" discovered on her spine, she was determined to get released all together.

However, Easter had passed some time ago so her "excuse" was a little dated. Knowing she would either be fined or have to serve some jail time to make up for her lack of service, I stepped in to, once again, solve her problems. She needed some kind of doctor note that was more recent... much more recent. Or else it just looked like she was not just lazy about her obligations, but also her health.

It was Thursday night and Hades was supposed to appear on Monday. I told her the best, and most reasonable thing, since she had no insurance, was to go to the free clinic. The West Hollywood was down the street and from the looks of it, very nice. I told her she should go first thing in the morning. Of course, Hades liked to sleep so first thing in the morning to her apparently meant 5 minutes before they closed. We walked in and were immediately denied service.

The lack of concern for her own welfare usually meant one of one thing: $. The only way to make it so the judge didn't laugh at her was to get her into an urgent care. I made the appointment for the next day (Saturday) and was promptly told there was a minimum $200 fee. I made the appointment anyway and 24 hours later my account was two bills less than it was when I made the call. Hades, as usual, offered to pay, but she also complained about constantly being overdrawn on her account. It was a nice gesture to offer to pay, but I also knew that's all it was.

Sunday night was a long night. She said she was too nervous to sleep, but I think it was the continuous Adderall consumption that made it impossible to enjoy any rest. You see, Hades no longer could be sustained on a quarter of the pill, she was up to a full high dosage at a time. I, however, was not so when I stayed up all night, I felt it.

The worst part preparing for her court visit wasn't the expense or making sure she was mentally prepared, it was the last minuteness of everything. She didn't know where her MADD class certificate was, which meant about two hours of ripping her pigsty of a condo apart... looking through every piece of paper laying around... twice.

I took her to court and since she was asking for a medical extension/ dismissal, all we could do was schedule a time to see the judge. The first opening they had was 8am, two days from now. All that frantic running around, not only was unnecessary, but was also going to repeat itself in 48 hours.

It was around 8pm Hades asked if I wouldn't mind going home, as she had to have two serious talks: one with Roommate for his lack of respect to her shithole and the other with Wacked Out Neighbor for also disrespecting her shithole. She blamed Whacked Out Neighbor's impromptu using-her-place-as-a-storage-room as to why her MADD paperwork went missing. At this point I was seriously beginning to dislike Roommate as this was probably the fourth time she was going to have this talk with him.

I was exhausted and was happy to go home and catch up on some needed sleep. She asked if I would take her dog, too. That's when the request of my departure felt weird. I agreed, picked up my things, and left.

As I made my way to my car, I decided to take my time on this one. I took the dogs on a long walk, drove up to McDonald's and hung out there a bit before making my way home. Trust between us was destroyed and I had all these wild fantasies of what her real agenda was this evening... Did she have plans to have someone else over or were these two talks necessary and really happening? Luckily as I drove back, she was home without any foreign cars parked out front.

"Whew," I thought to myself, "good girl."

I made a quick stop to get gas and as I reflected on how our relationship might actually build back to where it once was, Hades' black Volvo pulled into the stall next to mine. She hopped out, ran into the mini-mart, grabbed some snacks, exited the gas station, and hopped onto the 101. I was in shock.

She didn't even see me. Where was she going? What was she up to? I had to know. I jumped into my car and caught up with her. She exited Vine and turned left on Melrose.

"Artist Guy lives over here," I thought to myself. But then we passed his street. It was shortly after Western I hit the red and lost her.

To this day I have no idea where she went. FFPRMF was, at this point, living in a church somewhere where Melrose dead ends. I assumed she was going there to have a reunion not only with her girlfriend but also either G or Speed. For that moment, I thought, "The drugs can have her."

CHAPTER 27
Going 101 South

Any normal person in my situation would have done something about it. I, however, am not normal. She called me from the car the night of her adventures in lying to tell me she was getting a snack. At this point, we both knew she was lying, but I was falling back into a state of denial. "There was no way this was happening," I thought to myself as I circled the area as if I could hone into her phone call.

It was less than two weeks since the trust I had for her flew out the window and now here she was cruising down the 101 South going someplace for the night. As I drove around, trying to figure out where Hades could possibly be, I felt my well-being crawling into the back seat, where it decided to reside for a while.

"If I call her out," I thought, "she'll shut down, miss court, and go to jail." At this point I ceased being her boyfriend and morphed into a private investigator. I wanted to know what she was doing, so when I actually pointed fingers at her, I had all the facts.

I held my tongue and two mornings later drove her to court. She stood in front of a judge, showed him the $200 doctor's note I bought her, and he extended her community service to do office work at a non-profit drug rehabilitation center. On paper it was the best place to put Hades. She could quite possibly see the ramifications of people who devote their lives to drugs. However, deep in my gut, I knew this was not going to be good. It felt wrong and I knew it wouldn't turn out right.

On the way home, she sensed something was wrong. I'm good at hiding when something is bothering me, but she always knew when I was upset. We were a good match in that sense. Something rubbed me the wrong way, she knew almost immediately. It took her a couple days on this one, but once her court obligations were fulfilled, I guess I allowed myself to uncork that which was bottled.

I didn't tell her about the incident from two nights ago. I always wanted nothing more from her than just to come clean and admit things she did, even if they were horrible. I felt if she opened that door, we could ultimately be fixed. At the time, as much as I tried to rationalize her and the situation, it seemed like a reasonable request.

Instead of saying, "I know this, I know that," I simplified it to a hunch. I told her I had a feeling she was doing G again, that it was just a gut feeling. Just as I thought two days ago, the moment I said it, her walls went up, and she shut down. I had no proof that she was doing it, but I knew something was up. You don't lie to your boyfriend and hop on the 101 if nothing is going on. If it wasn't drugs, it was cheating... the drugs I could deal with, but I wouldn't date a cheater.

To me, cheating is not only the ultimate insult and injury, but severs everything. If you have needs outside of your monogamous relationship, just don't be in a relationship. At that point, there is no point. Something I always told her was, "If you need to be single, be single."

She denied using. She then told me that if I feel this way now and she wasn't using, she would never live the drugs down and there was nothing left for her. She "might as well be using if I was going to just accuse her of it anyway." That made me feel bad in many ways. The first was that she was partly right. If she wasn't using, and that's what I thought, then she would always be guilty. The sad thing here was, she was guilty of something, and if it wasn't drugs, then it was far worse.

If I made it sound like I knew something was up, I had so much faith in Hades that she would open up and admit to something. "Just give me that inch," I would think, "If you can just give me that much, I will do anything and everything to save what we have. Just give me an inch."

Unfortunately, Hades is metric.

CHAPTER 28
Dearly Departed

What the hell do I do? My friends at this point knew something was wrong. I wasn't sleeping. I wasn't eating. I started to lose weight and frankly looked like hell. Sadly, Hades was the only person that didn't notice. I guess draining my life-force was how she gained her strength.

Was it time to finally call it quits? As I asked myself this, my mother called me to tell me that her father, my grandfather, was suddenly days away from death. Did I want to go through a break-up and a death in the family at the same time? Now it was time for me to be selfish.

I told Hades of the situation and that I was going to have to go to Arizona on any given notice. I asked her to join me. She agreed. I was a bit taken aback by this as it seemed a bit selfless. She was offering to be there for me in a time of need.

Somewhere while all this was going on, her FFPRMF had set her up to meet with and shoot with a photographer that does a lot of Victoria Secret models. This was a huge step up for Hades' modeling career, however, the guy wanted to do a nude series with her. She agreed... without talking to or discussing it with me. Hades will always do what Hades does... and that's anything she wants. The time and date was set and before I knew it she was getting ready to go pose naked for another guy.

When I met her, she was clear about not doing nude work. However, much later on, I found out this wasn't her first nude shoot. I have since found out she did various nude shoots with various "photographers" she met on the internet.

With death and a funeral in the queue, I just didn't have the mental capacity to process all this. We had been, at this point, discussing moving in together and renting out her condo. Seemed like a logical step if I was going to just sweep everything under the rug, as apparently that's what I was doing. Hades did at one point go look at some apartments on a whim, which all things considered, was probably the most impressive and proactive thing she had done at this point in our relationship.

While she was off, having artistic nude photos taken of herself, I went to check out the place she found and it was nice. Too nice in fact and a place that I, as sole provider right now, couldn't afford. However, in another life, another time, it would have been a fantastic place to share with a significant other.

By this point my Grandfather had passed and Friday morning we were to drive out to Arizona. I had a eulogy to write and Hades had to go home and pack. She said she'd pack quick and then come back to my place to help me in any way she could.

She went home, via doing a drug deal on the way. At times to make a few quick bucks she became the middle man in selling various sorts of illegal substances. Once she got home, she called to tell me she had Roommate issues to deal with. This time Roommate was about to invite a half dozen friends over and she decided she had to stay the night at home to make sure this didn't happen. We all know how the last Roommate situation went, but she promised to be packed and be at my place first thing in the morning. I wanted to be in the car on the way to Phoenix by 11am.

That night as I wrote my Grandfather's eulogy, my thoughts went from sadness to anxiety. Around midnight, Hades responded to a text, which meant she was up. I decided to pop by.

I drove up to her place and no one was home. Hades, once again, defied my trust and spent the night somewhere she shouldn't have been... or at least somewhere she couldn't tell me she was.

To add insult to injury once again, she was unresponsive again until about late morning, which meant we would not leave on time. Hades, instead of packing as she said she was doing, was somewhere she wasn't supposed to be. That meant she had to go home in the morning to pack. She didn't arrive to my place until after 1pm (two hours after I wanted to leave) and even when she did arrive, she wasn't fully ready. My 11am planned departure was now 3pm.

The thing about Hades is she lost her brother when she was 22, which as she told it, changed her life in many ways. The loss still affects her entire family in ways I cannot even express. Being an observer, her brother's presence is still very, very active. If anyone should understand a death in the family, it should be Hades. She should have been there for her boyfriend. However, once again, she was MIA, most likely getting high, cheating, or both.

CHAPTER 29
Art is Art is Art

The drive to Arizona was, if nothing else, surreal. Hades sat shotgun in the rental car as I navigated through pre-rush hour traffic. Traffic on I-10 is much worse at 3pm than it would have been at 11am. As we made our way through Palm Springs, Hades began relentlessly sending and receiving text messages. She told me it was Nude Photography Guy who was in the process of retouching some of her images. Before I knew it, she was pulling up email after email on her iPhone. She passed the phone to me and there she was, in a very beautiful, artistic photo... completely naked. Her eyes and breasts burned a hole through me. Was this my future? My girlfriend constantly naked and forever immortalized into history. She told me when we were 80, I'd love to have these images stored away somewhere. Problem was, I wasn't 80, and these weren't just for my amusement, but apparently others as well.

Hades was beautiful and as far as art goes, these were gorgeous. You could even see the vulnerable side of her in the pictures. Like all women, Hades had insecurities, and something about these pictures made her feel even better about herself. That's a great thing, except during this ride. Besides constantly going back and forth via text with Nude Photography Guy, she was wearing a dress that kept slipping off her shoulder. Every five minutes or so, I had to tell her to put her boob away.

You read that right, we were driving down moderately busy I-10 and Hades' boob kept falling out of her dress. I have to deal with nude photos possibly going out to the world; I'm not going to deal with truckers ogling my girlfriend's breasts on a random Friday afternoon.

Remember, we are driving to Arizona to attend my Grandfather's memorial and now Hades is getting defensive because I don't want the populous of I-10 to see her exposed breast.

Before we left, Hades asked if I was feeling better. You see, I had texted her just before I popped by the night before. I told her I was feeling down while writing the eulogy and that call for help went unanswered. I envisioned her, somewhere she wasn't supposed to be, unable to respond because she couldn't talk to me in front of whomever she was with. I told her that to clear my head, I drove around town for a couple hours. She inquired where I went, I could tell she was probing and afraid I knew she wasn't home last night. I simply answered, "Everywhere," and left it at that. I wanted to call her out, but really needed her the next couple of days.

On the road she asked to hear my eulogy but before I could recite it to her, she again started texting Nude Photography Guy. The person I wanted here to support me, the shoulder I wanted to cry on, clearly was too enamored with herself to be there for me.

The entire drive I didn't just want, but needed her support, and all I could think about was, "Where were you last night?"

CHAPTER 30
Her Cup Runneth Over

We arrived at my mom's house in Phoenix around 11pm, roughly 5 hours late. The plan was to spend the night there, then drive the 2 hours to Tucson first thing in the morning. That was the plan.

We brought the dogs with us, and that was a bit of a shock to my mom, but ultimately I think that we were so late put everyone on edge. One thing led to another and next thing I know we're back in the car on our way to Tucson instead of spending time with my family.

For the most part, besides the acrimony, I actually preferred doing this. I was still tightening up the eulogy and this gave me more time to do it, as well as would give Hades a 2-hour head start on everyone the following day. We had a funeral to attend, and I did not want to be late. Two hours seemed like more than enough time to make sure she would be ready.

The day of the funeral, as expected, no matter how much you try to prepare, no matter how much you do for Hades, she always needs an extra 30 minutes. It was so ridiculous that there was regular time and Hades time, where I would tell her things started a half hour earlier, just so we wouldn't be late. She caught on to this quickly and soon we were running an hour late to things.

We were supposed to meet everyone at my Grandmother's, and then make our way to the funeral home. Something to note here, besides a brief moment meeting my mom once, Hades was being introduced to my family for the first time.

By the time we made it to the car, we were already late. We had to divert our plans, forego seeing everyone beforehand, and meet at the church. If it hadn't been for the pre-meet, we would have arrived late to my own Grandfather's funeral.

The rest of the day went well. Hades charmed my family in the way sociopaths are good at. Again, you must remember, Hades, if nothing else, had charisma and wit, which is why I stuck with her. She hid the bad stuff well, the good stuff, however was out in the open for everyone to see. I always told her she was a chameleon, with the ability to morph into whatever she needed to in order to make people enjoy her company.

That evening we went back to the hotel and drank more margaritas than I can remember. At this point it was just Hades and I enjoying each other's company, as we stared out at the dark desert sky.

I did drink too much and as we made it back to the room, I threw up. I laid down a little after midnight exhausted from a long day of family, funeral, and now intoxication. Hades said she'd be joining me in bed in ten minutes.

I woke up at 5am to Hades furiously texting. I asked her what was going on. She started to explain that FFPRMF was pissed that Nude Photography Guy offered to do a second shoot with Hades. I still can't figure out why this would set FFPRMF off and can only assume there were many other factors going into this argument. Over the next few days and weeks, this fight was going to turn into an all out war. However, at this moment, I felt very little support from Hades in any way, shape or form. Finally, I said, "We're here for me. My family. And you're up all night fighting with FFPRMF. I don't get it."

She said she felt bad about how she was acting, but this is when I realized, no matter what was happening in my world, be it life or death, there's not a enough room in Hades for my drama.

CHAPTER 31
Insane in the Membrane

All things considered, I couldn't help ignore that Hades did go to Arizona with me and spent three days with my family. It takes a lot to do that, I understand that much. We sat at my Grandmother's nursing home listening to stories of my Grandfather, who was a kind and gentle soul, and I just wanted all the bad things in this relationship with Hades to go away. There were so many perfect days where the crap felt like it didn't exist. At this moment, I was having one of those days. As my family's chatter rumbled around the a table, I secretly sent her a text: *I want to grow old with you.*

I meant it. I knew there were problems but I was sure they were fixable. Hades was damaged and I took on that knowledge from the beginning. Sure, I didn't realize just how dark her soul was, but it wasn't trying to figure out calculus. I saw the problems, some days ignored them; other days tried to figure them out, but at the end of the day, I saw a solution, a light at the end of the tunnel. Maybe I was just naive or simply hopeful, but in the moment, I had not just hopes and dreams, but the ability to achieve them, hell or high water.

A few days after we returned to Los Angeles, on the following Friday, Hades had an audition. She kept texting me her insecurities as she stood in a line of other beautiful women all up for the same part. I asked if she wanted to come over that evening, but she told me she had friend duty to do. Her Best Guy Friend recently lost a family member and needed someone to talk to about it, Hades, being the gracious woman she was, offered her platonic services.

It was this day that I finally, even via a text message, was able to see the lies unfolding as they happened. The rose colored glasses I had been opting to wear finally cracked. It was a surreal moment... a sad, but important day... and now I had to know for 100% that my gut was right.

Days before, I realized just how easy and just how cheap it was to rent a car. Using just my blackberry, I reserved a car for the evening. Was I about to do this? What had become of me? Although I just happened to see things before, this was the first pre-meditated and planned surveillance.

I picked up the car which cost me about $20 for the night and promptly drove to the Underworld that was Hades' domain. She was still home and even called me at one point asking me a few "do you know where this or that is" questions. I eventually parked across the street and just watched.

If there was ever a case for intelligent design, it was where Hades lived. Her place, sadly, was perfectly set-up to be watched: her car, every window in the place, as well as the front door to the building, all visible from where I sat. I stared at the little bathroom window for 30 minutes as she was doing what Hades did to get ready. Eventually a truck pulled up and a guy made his way to the intercom. Who was this? Was he here for Hades or just an innocent bystander? One thing was for certain, I didn't recognize him. He went inside and moments later I saw him sit down in Hades' living room. This was not her Best Guy Friend.

Hades, always one to run late, made him wait as I did too many times to count. They eventually left together in his truck; she even had her dog with her. I followed them down the 101 South, they went into downtown which was much further than Vine, so I hypothetically ruled him out from the gas station incident.

They eventually pulled into a parking garage and I waited outside. Somehow I lost them. I had an idea of who this was and was right. It turned out to be a friend whose name she mentioned before. We'll just call him White Trash Looking Actor. White Trash Looking Actor had a regular spot on a sitcom, a lesser known, lesser liked sitcom. His name came up whenever she needed acting advice, but whenever his name did arise, she mentioned how White Trash Looking Actor had a girlfriend and in exchange for acting tips, she advised him on his sinking relationship.

I went home and that numbness was starting to become a more permanent feeling. Once again I thought about my future and my mental health. I sent her a text, "I can't believe you're doing this." It was vague because I knew I'd chicken out and tell her it was meant for someone else. It took her about 30 minutes to call me. I was surprised she could. She usually compartmentalized me and the others, so I assumed he had no idea who I was. I was right, since when she called to see what I knew, I played dumb, and she quickly she said, "I gotta go," and hung up. I guess White Trash Actor Guy was returning.

Again, I was devastated yet blinded. I had never been so blatantly lied to. My mind just couldn't understand it and therefore refused to. It didn't make sense. Why tell someone you love them, if you're incapable of it?

Was this all just a game? If it was, I wasn't ready to fold just yet.

CHAPTER 32
The Passenger

I bought my ticket into Hades and now I felt like a unassuming passenger going for the ride of his life. I seemed to always be a victim of bad timing when it came to actually confronting Hades on her inconsistencies and lies. I hate using the word, "Victim," but for one reason or another, I always found my excuse to push things out even longer. I could have ended this all at the gas station and forced Hades to change her ways. Confused and lost, I let everything continue, and blamed happenstance. I wanted to save this girl, but watched like an innocent bystander as she not just corrupted what I thought we had, but continued to self-sabotage herself into an abyss.

What was it this time? Weeks before I started planning for Hades' birthday. She was inching towards the last year of her twenties and I wanted to give her a birthday that she wouldn't soon forget. Once again using that perfect hindsight like a new superpower, I realize something. Hades and I took so many trips together because it focused her on us, rather than the attention she could and would seek when she was in her element.

I purchased for us a 3-day cruise from Long Beach to Mexico. I didn't pour a lot of money into it, but I could confront her and probably toss that money away or I could do what I was getting really good at: procrastinate the inevitable. I opted once again for the painful route and let this ship stay on course.

Hades was a tough nut to crack, obviously a monogamous relationship was something she was incapable of, no matter how much she wanted it. I wish I was a Sociology major so I could excuse my actions, or in-actions, as case study.

I took the next few weeks to try and figure out if I was going crazy or if I was the only sane one in the room. I now know how conspiracy theorists feel trying to get others to comprehend what no one seems to understand. My girlfriend was blatantly lying to me but all her facts seemed to somehow check out. Was she that good or was I that insecure? The one thing I did know for sure was I was losing it.

As I tried to stay logical and be that self-proclaimed private investigator, all I was really doing was changing my seat on this trip to Crazytown. What's the difference between first class and coach when the plane is about to crash?

As we prepared for the trip, I expected Hades to run late. The boat disembarks at 5pm. I told her we had to be there by 2pm or else the boat would leave without us. We arrived, as I planned, at 3:30pm. This Harpy was completely non-functioning.

What made her late this time was as unusual as all the other times. The first was an interaction with the Police and Perverted Car Broker (another story, another time). Earlier that week, Old Music Guy apparently tiring of Hades antics sent her a scathing email. This day, the day Michael Jackson passed, she decided to forward on to me. Here are the good parts:

Hades,

Maybe I misinterpreted who you are. Maybe we should have just had a business arrangement where I propositioned you for sex. That could be okay and no one would have been misled. Sex at least is honest.

I moved on from you as a friend after our first evening. You blew off a multi-millionaire, someone who would have helped your career, taken you around the world, markedly improved your lifestyle, given you an honest relationship and a place of prestige among Hollywood and for what?

I started dating a girl, she's only 25 while the years are catching up with you aren't they. The most annoying aspect of my time with you however is that you'd use my friendship with FFPRMF as the lamest excuse I've ever heard for you to get out of a relationship we weren't even in. I can't even call it a friendship.

All you've done is make a really bad enemy and you don't need any in my town. You don't know what you missed. Yeah, I'm not Brad Pitt but your not Jessica Biel, Megan Fox or even the beautiful FFPRMF. You really blew it!!! Lastly....Well there is no lastly. I think you get the message.

Old Music Publisher Guy

I wasn't sure how she expected me to react to this. My first comment was, "This sounds more like a scorned lover than anything else.". She denied that and only offered that on their last meeting he attempted to kiss her, a move she thwarted. What she wanted from me was sympathy. Her birthday was 2 days away, we were leaving for a trip this afternoon, and she was completely delusional about how I was supposed to react. Old Music Guy was finally gone, but what was he leaving exactly.

I was days away from putting the finishing touches on my emotional walls. No longer was I going to let this stuff in. I was cutting myself off and finally preparing for what had to be done.

After the cruise, of course.

CHAPTER 33
Good Mourning!

Hades' brother died in a freak accident almost a decade ago. Her and her family still talk about him almost daily. It's a sad cause of events that ripped the union apart. She told me many stories about him and personally I think he would have been a great person to meet. He seemed rather remarkable and was apparently the glue that held the family together. When he left, and did so tragically, the bonds between parents and children evaporated. They all seemed to go their own path trying to deal with the loss in any way they could: good or bad.

The death of her brother soon put Hades into a drug binge which led her to rehab by her early 20's. This was something she told me about the first night we met. I knew that her late brother had a remarkable place in his heart for Hades. When he passed he left her everything. She was grateful to use the money to buy a condo so that she, "would never have to rely on a man." She also admitted that she snorted about $100,000 of the inheritance on cocaine. At least she never had to use her body to score her drug of choice.

She had a condo with a mortgage and a delinquent homeowner's association debt, but she at least had a home. She was broke now, but the roof over her head that her brother provided, even deceased, was always there for her. I knew the upcoming anniversary of his birth was going to be a rough one. Hades warned me in advance to be prepared for the worst. I worked from home that day as she slept in.

When she finally woke up, she decided she wanted to be alone and have a quiet celebration for her brother's life. I told her that I would be there for her when she either needed me or returned. Her plan was to drive up to Santa Barbara to reflect on old times, both good and bad.

Hades drove off and within a few minutes left me the following message:

> *Hey, it's Hades. I just wanted to tell you that I love you. Um, yeah... I have so much fun with you. I love you; you're the best. I really, really, really, really, really do. I'll talk to you later. Bye.*

Hours went by as I worried about Hades' mental health. How was she taking this day? Was it sad? Nostalgic? Peaceful? All I could do was let her know that I was there for her. Later she texted me saying that she might spend the night at a girlfriend's in Santa Barbara. In a normal, healthy relationship, this would be fine. This is why trust is the most paramount part of any relationship. When it's gone, it's gone. When she told me that, the alarm bells went off.

Eventually, Hades did come home. Over a glass of wine, she told me about where in Santa Barbara she went to reflect on the life and on the memories of her brother. It was sad, yet sweet. Truly interested, I asked questions about her day, all of which she not just answered, but in great detail. It sounded like she had a nice day with the ghosts of the past.

A week later we were sitting on the couch and I looked over her shoulder and noticed her writing to an agent. In her email, she stated, "*I met you last Thursday on the set of White Trash Looking Actor's TV show.*" But, last Thursday she told me she was in Santa Barbara.

That's how I found out that the day she was supposed to be in Santa Barbara remembering her dead brother, she was actually in town, hanging out with White Trash Looking Actor. The was the by far the lowest I've ever seen anyone go.

CHAPTER 34
6 Months, Time Served

It was right after the cruise that our 6 month anniversary was fast approaching. Yes, these stories fit in the time span of one half of one year. Hard to believe myself sometimes. Living it was an emotional roller coaster split between imagined happiness and total despair.

Two days previous, Hades and I got into an argument. I believe it was over her homemade audition tape for some show she was trying out for. The show wanted an Olivia Munn type, so Hades secluded herself in the bathroom and did two takes of a script I wrote for her that night. I was fast asleep and when I woke up the next morning, she asked for my input. She had been up for at least 24 hours when she made the video audition. My initial comment was, "it's good but you're exhausted, and it shows." And, even worse, she was planning to stay up until the actual audition later that day.

She was pissed at my honesty. Apparently, as her boyfriend, I was the only one not allowed to give her constructive criticism. I was upset that she didn't want a critique, just the words that she wanted to hear. I soon morphed into the guy that told her all her work was "great" even if it wasn't.

During our day apart, I brought up the looming half year anniversary. She unknowingly made plans which she said she would cancel.

By the Monday of the 6th, all the hard feelings were again forgotten and we had a lovely dinner at the restaurant where we first met. Afterward, as we walked to the car, I stopped her at the spot of our first kiss to recreate that moment, and then we parted.

The plan was that she was going to go home, get clothes for tomorrow, and come back to my place. That was the plan. Specifically she needed clothes for the next day to come to my office and participate in a table read. A table read, as you may guess, is just a handful of actors reading a piece of written work so the writer can hear it read. About 3 hours after we rekindled that first kiss, she called me asking what clothes she should pack for the next day. It was baffling since a table read has no dress code and is simply super casual/come as you are. Even more confusing was Hades participated in one of them before, so this wasn't something new to her. She lashed out at me when I said for her to wear anything she wanted. Our anniversary at this moment was ruined.

This is one of those times the Borderline "splitting" came into play. One moment she was happy and proud of our six months; the next minute she cannot stand to talk to me like a rational human being. I attempted to save the night by heading to her place, however, that was apparently the wrong thing to do. Once that Border-line is crossed, it's impossible to step back. All you can do it distance yourself and wait for the Personality Disorder to shift back to normal. I ended up picking out an outfit for her and leaving in a huff. I was exhausted from this. I went home; I went to bed.

The next morning Hades was MIA. An hour before the start of the read, Hades called to tell me she had been up all night crying, therefore she wasn't going to attend the read. All things considered, I was pretty good at not getting mad at Hades, but if one thing got to me, it was her unprofessionalism. If she wants to be late to each and every meeting or audition that is for her, so be it, but do not affect my work, especially when a room full of people are counting on you. After I told her how rude this behavior was, she got in the car and made her way... She was 45 minutes late.

She read her lines unenthusiastically and only spoke to me when her character was required to do so. Afterward she barely said good-bye as she headed out to what might have been another shady photo shoot which required implied nudity... for which she was paid zero dollars, zero cents.

CHAPTER 35
Keyless Entry

It was a random Friday night and we were hanging out at my place. We were talking about ordering dinner and watching a movie, when out of the blue Hades tells me she's having roommate problems again. At this point, Roommate seemed to be making life difficult for Hades. It was such an odd thing since he was a very quiet guy, kept to himself, if he even stayed home. At this point he was spending most of his time elsewhere. When I would come over, you'd see him maybe 5 minutes, if at all. He would enter, say hello, go to his room, shut the door, and pretty much disappear. From what Hades described, he was always inviting multiple people over, destroying her property, never pitching in, and constantly a problem. Aside from being late on rent and having to break-up the payments sometimes, he didn't really bother me all that much and was a pretty nice guy.

This night was like any other nights, but Hades just had to get home. She was jittery, anxious, and the situation wasn't going to fix itself, and for reasons I couldn't figure out, she needed to fix them immediately. She didn't invite me to join, and like many roommate situation nights, I knew there was something more up her sleeve.

I asked her if she was going to come back after, to which she replied, "No." I walked her to her car and told her, "Good luck with the roommate." She promptly left and in no time she called me in a panic.

"What's wrong?" I asked.

"I dropped my keys down the elevator shaft."

Good thing she couldn't see my face since I was rolling my eyes. This girl, no matter how much she tried, just could not function. Even stranger was she was locked out.

"Where's your roommate?" I inquired, "Can't he let you in?"

"He's not here."

My suspicions were even more piqued as I said, "I'm on my way."

I immediately drove over to her with some tools and found her sitting with her dog outside her apartment. Added onto the anxiety and jitters, she looked exhausted. I went to work on the door and about 10 minutes later, we were inside her condo. Some time before we met, she lost the keys to her deadbolt, which meant she never secured anything more than the simple knob lock. She was thankful that night, but of course later would turn the fact that I could pick the simplest of locks as my being "scary and dangerous."

She tried to explain how Roommate was supposed to meet her there, however, was somewhere up near Valencia (a good 45 or more minutes away). It absolutely made no sense, as Roommate wasn't so stupid to just stand her up like that. However, she insisted he did.

What made perfect sense was within a few minutes of our settling in, Hades told me that Once Famous Video Vixen was on her way over. She complained of the pop-ins because Video Vixen always came in, used her bathroom, hung out for 2 minutes and then would promptly leave. She said this weirded her out since Video Vixen had genital herpes.

Once Famous Video Vixen did exactly as Hades described: She walked in, said hello, went to the bathroom, came out, said good-bye and left. It was odd and it took me some time to realize that this was how Hades bought drugs. Sadly, the Once Famous Video Vixen was now just a common drug dealer. Hades hid money in a box in her bathroom and like an addicts magic trick, she'd open it to find it replaced with whatever fix she needed.

I always thought Hades was a riddle, wrapped in a mystery, inside an enigma; but perhaps there was a key to unraveling everything. Unfortunately it wasn't with those at the bottom of the elevator shaft. To solve the mysteries of this Harpy, I would have to continue my venture deeper into the next Circle of Hell.

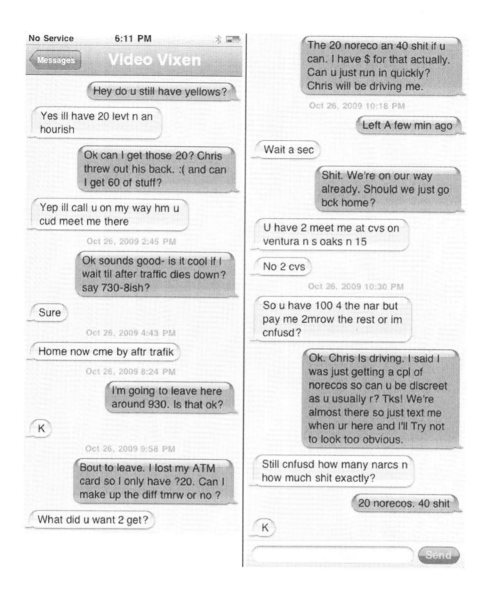

CHAPTER 36
Failure to Launch (Part I)

Around the time I met Hades, I opened a new company. My life felt pretty good at that time. My career moving forward and the girl of my dreams at my side. It was a fantastic feeling having a great business partner on one end, a great life partner on the other. As you know, things went downhill on the personal side really fast.

It was the middle of July and I was throwing a launch party for the company. It was an exciting time. Everyone in my life, business and personal, would all be there to celebrate. Hades told me how excited she was for me.

Weeks earlier Hades agreed to do some freelance photo work for this woman who was putting together some webseries. Whatever she was doing, it sounded really unstable. She was creating a webseries but instead of shooting video, she went around town having Hades take pictures of her acting like some pseudo-diva. I was half expecting this woman to claim to have invented Post-Its. Whatever. Although unpaid, it made Hades feel productive, and when Hades felt good, it made everything go so much smoother.

Hades spent half the day leading up to the party snapping pictures of the Broke Diva. To make Hades more comfortable I told her to feel free to add some of her friends to the party list, including Broke Diva. Broke Diva had no car, so half of Hades "photo assignment" was carting B.D.'s ass around.

The party was slated to go from 7pm-12am. I spoke to Hades at 6pm as I was getting ready, and she assured me she'd be there at 8pm to be by my side.

8pm: Friends, acquaintances, and colleagues all came up to congratulate me.

9pm: People started to ask where Hades was.

10pm: I started really making excuses. A little after this, Hades called freaking out that she was so late. At one point, I thought she said, "Your friends are probably wondering where I am." Over the loud music, I wanted to clarify that Hades was being empathetic. But what she actually said was, "My friends are probably wondering where I am." So yes, it was still about her friends, all my people be damned.

She was finally on her way, so I told her I would search her friends out, just happy she was going to actually show up. I found her Female Musician Friend and soon after learned that Hades forgot something, went back home, and lost her keys in the process. Now she was waiting for a cab. There I was, at my own party, entertaining Hades' friends.

It was at this moment I turned white. Female Musician Friend recently returned from overseas and told me that it was only yesterday that she had seen Hades. That was interesting since two nights before Hades and her were supposedly hanging out. Hades told immense details of this hang, including how she was too drunk to drive home so Female Musician Friend drove her while FMF's roommate followed in Hades' car. Again, specific events of things that never, ever happened.

What was most interesting wasn't the lies themselves, but the intricate details that went into them. Here I was learning that my girlfriend had once again blatantly lied to me, disappeared for an evening, used this friend as her excuse (without telling her), and ended up somewhere else.

Four hours after the party started, at 11pm, Hades made her entrance. She didn't come alone, she was sure to bring her dilated eyes and erratic behavior with her. Something was off and instead of being apologetic to me, I could tell that the night was just about to get interesting.

CHAPTER 37
Failure to Launch (Part II)

Hades was most likely drunk, high or both when she finally walked through the door. Although four hours after I arrived and approximately one hour before the whole party would end, she was finally there. I immediately pulled her where I wanted her to be all night, which was by my side. Within a few minutes she asked if she could go say hi to her old boss. I was fine with it, I wanted Hades to use this opportunity to mingle and make friends with some of my friends. Unfortunately by this time most of the people I wanted to introduce her to had already left.

The moment that Hades was anxious about was meeting my ex who had become like a sister to me. The meeting was inevitable and to preempt the awkwardness, Hades befriended her on Facebook and they soon went back and forth.

Soon after their meeting, Hades pulled me aside and asked me, "What did she mean by that?"

"What?" I asked.

"I'm glad you're doing better."

I didn't know what that meant. I told Hades I'd go see what was implied. Hades asked me not to. I agreed, but I could tell Hades was not about to drop it as she was already huffing around. Remember, I'm still in a state of shock having just learned that Hades lied to me two nights ago.

Soon after this my Ex came up to say good-bye to me. I took this moment to ask her if she said what Hades accused her of. She denied it and related whatever she did say to something in their Facebook exchange. I was ready to blow it off as a mis-communication misheard over loud music and alcohol. Hades was not.

Hades, arms and legs tightly crossed, was sitting on the couch with her Female Musician Friend. They were talking about going to the Roosevelt after my party. At this point, I was five hours deep and all I really wanted to do was go home with my girlfriend. Maybe even get to the bottom of her mysterious disappearance 48 hours ago.

At some point in this conversation, I told Hades about the mis-communication. She felt betrayed that I went back on my word about not getting into whatever transpired between my ex and her. She even made some comment to her friend about me, "being in the dog house."

We made our way to the Roosevelt when she started the fight. This is when I decided if we were going to argue, we might as well argue about something real, and I said, "Why do you lie to me?"

She want quiet as I asked again.

"Because it's easier," she said in a monotonous, disassociating breath.

I revealed to her that unknowingly her friend sold her out. I asked where she was two days ago. She said she stayed home and just wanted to be alone. I pried deeper and found out White Trash Looking Actor came over to tell her about things FFPRMF had been saying about her.

"Are you cheating on me?" I asked.

"No."

"Then what do you do on these nights when you can't tell me what you're doing? Hanging out with people you can't tell me about?"

"Drugs," was her simple and to the point reply.

The fighting continued. We were supposed to go to Vegas the next day, which she was quick to back out of. I told her I was going without her then.

We diverted from the Roosevelt and ended up at her place. I was ready to watch her go in without me as the fighting had continued. Eventually I stopped yelling as did she. She asked me to come up. We laid on her bed, discussing the issue, while staring at the ceiling.

I asked about the lost evening wanting information that would help me understand. She prodded me about things that didn't really matter. She tried to turn the tables many times over, but the fact of the matter was, she was caught, and when Hades is caught and backed into a corner, she'll try everything to flip it, but ultimately she knows she has nowhere to go, nowhere to hide.

She became apologetic, sympathetic, and, as much as I wanted to believe, sincere. We talked it out. Drugs were an issue from day one, but also disclosed. I knew about the substance abuse getting into this relationship, yet I steered right in. That was my choice and I had to understand it. If she was being honest now, and I still wasn't sure if she was, I couldn't leave her just because of the drugs. The lying was a different story. If that continued, and I warned her, I would leave.

I forgave her and we decided to go to Sin City as planned. As we drifted off, we agreed that over our trip, we'd secretly get married.

CHAPTER 38
Cantaloupe

We woke up the next day with Vegas on our minds. Hades had a quick photo shoot, one of which would later turn out to be implied nudity where she was paid, I believe, $60. As she dropped her top, I was dropping off my dog at the sitter's. The plan was to leave as early as possible, which in Hades' mind, was that evening. I wanted to beat rush hour but Hades was coming down with a sore throat, so she was slow to pack.

Part of the talk the night before was how Hades excused her lies because that's how she "was raised." She said her mother planted the seed in her head that lying to others is best, including to your significant other, if it kept everyone happy. If Hades wanted to do drugs, she would tell me she was hanging out with a girlfriend, to keep the peace. Not acceptable to my standards, but I tried to understand.

Hades asked if I would talk to her sister so she could back-up her story. While chatting with her sis, Hades divulged that we were planning on eloping in the next 24-48 hours. Then Hades handed the phone to me...

For the next 20 minutes, I listened to Hades' sister warn me beyond belief that I was making the biggest mistake of my life. The sister tried to pound into my head that she was once like Hades, and now on her third marriage, she was finally learning from her mistakes. She told me Hades would need years of therapy and pounds of medications to fix all that ailed her. She said Hades would continue to lie to me, without remorse, without guilt, and, sadly, without regret. She knew this because this is what she did and finally after seeking rehab and psychiatric help, she was finally mending her own ways.

What Sister didn't know was Hades was listening to every word of warning.

I sat there and listened; I was unsure of how to even respond. After the run almost equal to that of a sitcom without commercials, Hades took the phone and started telling her sister how inappropriate and unfair this one-sided conversation was.

Hades went into the other room and I listened to her try and defend herself. She reiterated that the purpose of the call was to reinforce how they grew up with a mother that enforced lying. How dare she twist it into this warped cautionary tale to the man not only willing to put up with the bullshit but say, "I do" to the age old question "better or worse, richer or poorer, in sickness and in health, for as long as we both would live."

Hades finally ended the call and slowly walked back into the living room. She looked at me with her pale green eyes and sadly said, "You don't want to marry me anymore, do you?"

I raised my head and said, "I don't care what your Sister said. We're going to Vegas. We're getting married." I wished I would have ended that with, "God himself couldn't stop this marriage," but I didn't, because that would have been too classic.

CHAPTER 39
Betting Against the House

We were on the road, Vegas bound, around 10pm on this Friday night. A buddy of mine set us up for two nights at Planet Hollywood. As the dark interstate welcomed us on our equally unknown futures, we talked about our soon to be nuptials.

Hades' smile brightened the entire car, as she giddily kept saying, "We're gonna be married." I was excited and worried at the same time. I felt like vows would finally get Hades to shape up, change her ways, and ultimately be the wife I wanted. But, what if they didn't? We made a pit stop on the way to pick up bridal magazines and dog food. Hades never attempted to find a dog-sitter so her Beagle was jokingly going to be our witness.

Hades was happy to forgo a wedding dress until we would have a real wedding sometime the following year, but for now all she wanted was a veil. I told her she could have anything she wanted.

On the way, she complained of her sore throat that was getting worse the further we traveled. By the time we made it to Planet Hollywood, snuck in her dog, and finally checked-in, she needed something for the pain. I ordered her some food and walked the few blocks to the nearby CVS. I picked up as many different types of sore throat medication I could find.

We soon passed out around 5am talking about wedded bliss. A few hours later, Hades, in tears, woke me. Her sore throat had exacerbated into something much worse. She said she was in the most severe pain she had ever experienced. She needed to be taken to the emergency room.

The health insurance Hades had was supplied by her parents and restricted to California. After being transferred four times and having Kaiser Permanente on the phone for 30 minutes, they finally authorized her to go to a Vegas hospital. I drove her to the ER as quickly as I could. She was in too much pain to even swallow so she kept spitting her saliva into a cup. Triage said she'd have to wait but before long she was being taken back. I had to wait behind.

Eventually Hades came out with three prescriptions and a diagnosis of Strep Throat, "one of the worst cases the ER doctor had ever seen." We picked up her high dose Ibuprofen, Vicodin, and an anti-inflammatory and went back to the hotel. By this time, the shot they put in her butt, helped ease the pain. She apologized for not being the glowing bride-to-be, but if the next day went okay, we could still make it down the aisle.

The next 48 hours, Hades, for the most part, slept. She'd wake up long enough to eat, take her meds, and pass back out. The only time I wasn't by her side was when I was getting her soup and/or sandwiches from downstairs.

As she slept, I knew she needed an extra day to recover, so I went down to put my card on file to cover a third day. I walked back into the room, she was wide awake, and asked me if I had been going through her phone. At any point I could have, but didn't, so as much as I had been caring for the sick girl, I was really insulted being asked such a question. It made me wonder what might be in there to see, but I knew if there was anything, I would be forced to leave her.

I thought the worst was over, as Hades was on the mend, but on the third morning, the day we were to head back home, I awoke to Hades vomiting blood.

CHAPTER 40
Numerology FTW!

Let's take a brief break from Las Vegas for a moment. As you might be able to guess, vomiting blood isn't a quick fix. You can't just hop in the car and hope it takes care of itself... because like Hades, nothing was ever easy. In the meantime, as I gather all the memories of a Las Vegas wedding that didn't happen, I shall share with you something more in the realm of the metaphysical.

Hades was really into Tarot readings when we first met and soon enough everything in our relationship was being judged by pentacles, cups, swords, and wands. Hades loved any excuse to randomly pull out three cards which signified our past, our present and our future. Unfortunately, any time we were fighting, Hades would go into the bedroom and after an hour or so, return with three cards and the "How to Read Tarot" book. When she did that, I always knew what was coming. Like a child with a stuffed animal and security blanket, Hades would come out and plop herself down on the floor. She would then ask a variation of the same question:

"What are you hiding from me?"

A few times she would ask this when I knew she was lying to me, and sitting on information trying to call her out. It was creepy. The first time was the trip to Tucson. Although my grandfather's funeral overshadowed her and FFPRMF's spat, she still had time to question her spirit guide about what was wrong with me. This was a mind game tactic I had never experienced before.

Later, Hades started to get into Numerology. She always talked about being a "Six." When you add all the numbers in her birth date: month, date and year, then keep adding the numbers together until you had a single digit, she was a six. For example, Hitler was born on April 20, 1889. 4+2+0+1+8+8+9=32, then 3+2=5. Hitler is a 5.

Another important Numerology number is just adding the month and date. Hitler was 4+2+0=6. Like Hitler, Hades was, also and again, a 6. Hades was also born in the 6th month of the year.

If you've been paying attention, so far Hades is a 6 and a 6 and a... 6? I'm not a religious man, but...

Month, date and year=6
Month and year=6
Month of birth=6
Born on this day of week=6
Letters in her name (first and last)=6
Letters in her name (first, middle and last)=6
Letters in her name (last)=6
Letters in her nickname=6

Which bring us to the obvious Revelation and Armageddon conclusion:

666

CHAPTER 41

"Did You Eat Any Rotten Food?" (Vegas, Part II)

I awoke to find Hades with blood coming out of both ends. She complained she was now in the worst pain of her life. She curled up in the fetal position and cried as I waited for an alien to burst through her stomach. The pain from the strep throat was nothing at this point and now Hades couldn't stand, walk, or move. The only thing she was capable of was getting into the bathroom to hemorrhage some more.

Soon I found myself once again talking to the wonderful admins and nurses at Kaiser Permanente. This was Hades' California based insurance company, who I had to talk to to get prior authorization so I could get her into a hospital stat. 45 minutes later, I called her an ambulance.

We were staying in a VIP room at Planet Hollywood, and once you call an ambulance, the 911 operator calls the hotel to send up someone from hotel security to come sit with you while you wait. Before I knew it they were knocking on the door. I quickly had to stuff the Beagle into the 5'x 5' bathroom. Las Vegas Hotel Security must see some weird stuff, but for some reason they are too polite to just ask the obvious questions. Instead, our Security Guy kept doing a dance asking if Hades had, by any chance, maybe ingested something she might not normally (including rotten food). On any other given day, the answer would have probably been, "yes." Strangely enough, Hades was genuinely sick.

The paramedics arrived and took her vitals, looked her over, and suggested I just take Hades to the Urgent Care around the corner. They put her in a wheelchair, helped me get her into the car, and off we went. Eventually I was allowed back and the doctor informed me they were not equipped to deal with whatever it was Hades had. She had to be transferred to a hospital.

I followed the ambulance to the wonderful Sunrise Hospital, about 30 minutes away. Hades was admitted, taken back, and soon I was in Curtain Area Three with her. In this particular section there were five beds in one tight area. To get to Hades' bed, I had to walk through two other curtain areas... most pleasant. With us were:

-The old man who had to be told, *"Get your finger out of there! It's full of bacteria!"*
-The young girl with Down Syndrome that was prone to seizures.
-The guy that kept yelling that he was going to kill everyone in the ER.
-The old lady that shot herself in the leg.

All class acts, I can tell you. It was a miserable hospital, but luckily Hades had an amazing nurse that did every thing she could to make her comfortable. There was an early prognosis of gallstones, but eventually the ER Doctor that barely spoke English ruled that out. He also ruled out Hades, because Kaiser Permanente decided that Sunrise, a private hospital, was not for her, and she had to be transferred yet again.

After the immense painkillers finally kicked in and knocked Hades unconscious, I had this mental picture of as we left the hotel, the Do Not Disturb sign fell off the hotel room door. Which meant being 12am, the dog, at this point, was found. As Hades lie sleeping, I rushed back to Planet Hollywood, parked, ran up to the room, opened the door... The room had been cleaned, the lights were set to "mood," and there laid the little Beagle sprawled out on the turned down bed. Dogs were not allowed in the hotel, but apparently Housekeeping thought she was cute enough to let her stay.

I packed Hades a bag, rushed back to Sunrise, to find Hades still sleeping. Kaiser called me to arrange Hades' transfer to yet another hospital. At 3am I watched Hades get loaded up into another Ambulance.

Current Tally: Las Vegas Hospitals 3
                Urgent Care 1

CHAPTER 42
Say, "Cheese!" (Vegas, Part III)

The final hospital, happily, happened to be the nicest. Hades was somehow admitted en route and was taken straight from ambulance to her room. One thing I failed to mention here, something I never did tell Hades, was sometime in the last 24 hours I had been infected with her sore throat. Although it was killing me, I didn't have time to be sick. Maybe we hadn't yet exchanged our secret vows, but *in sickness and in health* was constantly on my mind. It was at this moment it occurred to me that as a partner, it didn't just mean be there for her when she is sick; I had to be there for her even when I am sick.

All through the night Hades' electronic IV monitor kept going off and only about 2 of the last 36 hours did I actually get a chance to sleep. There was one thing looming behind all this, a Beagle and an impending 11am check-out at Planet Hollywood. The VIP status had run out and I had to get over there. Once again, her pain meds kicked in, and I was off.

I gathered our bags and dog as I found a hotel near the hospital. It wasn't for me, but I had to put the Beagle somewhere. I felt horrible as the little puppy was getting very little attention and after the hotel transfer and a quick walk, I had to leave the canine alone once again.

Arriving back at the hospital, Hades was minutes away from being woken up to get a blood draw. Timing and medication allowed me to be there when she drifted off and again as she came to. A few hours later, she would be taken down for testing. While a camera was being slid down her throat, I sat down in the empty hospital cafeteria and ate the best grilled cheese sandwich of my life.

Hades was given a diagnosis: a grapefruit sized ulcer was tearing her apart from the inside-out. Besides altering her diet, going on acid reducing meds, and getting some rest, nothing else was necessary. As she rested, I sat by her side, read to her, and at the end of the day, did everything in my power to show Hades that I was there for her.

The hospital monitored Hades through the night and at the end of the next day discharged her. We picked up a bland Subway sandwich, laughed a bit at the experience, and rejoined the Beagle at the Quality Inn. I could finally relax knowing Hades was feeling better and after tomorrow's sunrise, her, the Beagle and I would be on our way home.

For better or worse, we never exchanged vows on this trip. We simply chalked it up as an inconvenience. But now, I think we are both thanking divine intervention.

CHAPTER 43
A House of Cards

We returned from Vegas, Hades was ordered by me to relax. Back in reality, there was a situation brewing in Hades' life, one that I was about to become immersed in. We might not have been husband and wife but we were partners in this life, and we had to figure the tough parts out together, or else flounder alone.

Hades, now out of work a half a year, the unemployment checks weren't enough to cover her daily expenses plus all the larger bills. Her mortgage was two months behind and her Homeowner's Association dues hadn't been paid long before she lost her job. Her condo had about four liens from the HOA and foreclosure was becoming eminent.

The easy solution was for us to consolidate and move in together. I tried for some time to get her to move in with me and rent out her place, but as it was in shambles, it was going to be impossible to find any kind of tenant. I wanted to live with her, I just didn't want to live in her filth. The only way to get this done was to get rid of my apartment, move into her condo, fix it up, then for us to move together somewhere else. Basically, suck it up and hopefully by the end of the year, we could move into a new place together. I had become accustomed to compromising in this relationship, so why change now?

This was a 6-month plan, and the only way to get it done was for us to work together. Two days after we returned from Vegas, I drove us to Hades' place with the sole duty and desire to clean. I started with her bedroom. In 4 hours time, I filled up just as many kitchen sized garbage bags. There were cans, bottles, and trash in every square inch of that room. While she rested on the couch, I went through paperwork, receipts, organized pictures, tossed old fast food bags, and uncovered old dog and cat poop in parts of the carpet that hadn't been seen in weeks, if not months.

It was quite a task and her room was just the beginning. Everything in the place needed either repainting, scrubbing, or simply updating. As I finished up the bedroom, scrubbing every fiber of carpet, I thought about putting in my 30-day move-out notice. I looked at the clean room and was hopeful that in 6 months we could really have her place looking brand new.

I had no idea the chain of events that were about to occur.

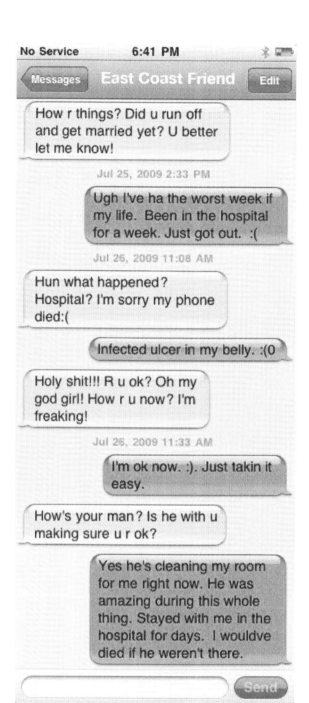

CHAPTER 44
The Streets of San Francisco

Hades and I were getting ready for a trip to San Francisco to visit a friend of hers. By getting ready, I mean I was packing while Hades did anything but. The night before Hades decided she needed to take her computer in for repair, so I offered to take the Beagle downtown so her Best Guy Friend could watch her.

I finished packing, went to bed, and when I awoke around 7am I walked toward the living room. I expected to see Hades crashed on the couch, completely unpacked. However, that's not what I found. Hades was wide-awake, having been up all night, her suitcase was in the middle of the living room (empty), and she sat on the couch attempting to thread a sewing machine.

"Whatcha doin'?" I asked.
"Trying to figure this thing out," she said.
"How's that coming?"
"I can't figure it out."

"Have you packed?"
"Not yet. Wanted to do this first."
"You think we'll leave on time?"
"Of course."

The sewing machine was an impulse buy a couple months before and besides the night she bought it, she had yet to even look at it, let alone figure out how it worked. But on this day, when Hades had to pack for a three day trip to visit her Girlfriend, she decided to take on this task.

Our flight was to depart in the early afternoon. The cab arrived at the time I told Hades to be ready, which it then waited outside for 30 minutes, meter running. There was no way we were ever going to make it and as we pulled up to the airport just as our plane was leaving, we were forced to wait and fly stand-by on the next flight.

We arrived in San Francisco, two hours behind schedule, and as we were just about to meet one of her best girlfriends, she decided to tell me that she, at one time, almost kissed Artist Guy. My heart dropped and as her friend walked up, I was unable to get anything more from her. I sat there, smiling, listening and conversing like a good boyfriend should. Little did Hades know, I had spoken to this friend on several occasions before. This friend worked at a jewelry store and we hatched a plan for Hades to not only reveal her ring size, but also to pick out options for her future engagement ring.

Finally, we departed her girlfriend and went back up to our room to talk. Hades denied anything but the near kiss. She said during one of their late nights in the studio, it came close, but that was it. It was here I asked what exactly was going on with all the guys lingering in her life, especially White Trash Looking Actor.

I finally called her out on all her lies. Basically, she told me, she lied so she could do drugs, namely Speed. I grilled her with questions for probably two hours, until she swore on her dead brother's name that she was telling me the truth.

I told her, based on that, I believed her and we would use this night to grow stronger. Of course the out-of-the-blue confession seemed more like a game to toy with my emotions as later I found out more was going on than just a near kiss. Why confess to anything if you're going to hold back? Also, this meant she was okay swearing on her Dead Brother's name to make people believe her lies. She clearly had no shame.

Side note: It was also on this trip that she showed me the park where she bought cocaine from a homeless guy.

CHAPTER 45
Are You Listening?

As you may have guessed, by this point in the relationship, the trust I had for Hades, for lack of a better word, was gone. In fact, even while cleaning her room, I compared every receipt's day and time with where she said she was at the time. I had been saving every text from her for pretty much this purpose. There were a few instances where she appeared to not be where she claimed to be.

Over the course of our relationship, I think the most saddening of these was once she told me she decided to attend an AA Meeting. She was given community service at a rehab center, but instead of AA, I later found the receipt that showed she was buying Vodka at the liquor store near her house nowhere close to the facility she was posted. I had previously showered her with praise for attending that non-existent meeting.

One August morning, I was leaving for work and Hades asked if I trusted her enough to watch my dog for the day. I did not, but I wanted to. So I left the dog in her care and trembled every time my phone rang, expecting the worst. Hades emailed and texted throughout the day home alone and bored, so I decided to cut out of work early. When I arrived home, I found her on the phone with an old friend.

Throughout the day all she wanted was for me to come home and now that I was there, I was patiently waiting for her to get off the phone. She openly talked about me to this friend, an aspiring director currently living in New Orleans. At one point, I ran down to the car, and when I came back, she was behind closed doors in the bathroom. Now this is where a normal, healthy relationship would be nice, however, we were too far down the rabbit hole. I did not, for life or death, trust this woman.

Curious, I wanted to know if she was still on the phone and if she retreated to privacy because she was talking to someone else or if maybe she just wanted to vent about me. That's when I put my ear to the opposite wall. On the other side of the plaster, I heard mumbling but no idea what was being said. I moved away, feeling sick to my stomach at what I had become, but within minutes I was back, ear pressed once again to the wall. This time, I heard... nothing.

I backed away this second time to see Hades standing opposite me, a quizzical look on her face. Yup, I was caught with my ear to the wall. I have to say, this was by far the most humbling and comical moment of my life, yet all too serious. She hung up the phone and an argument started. I admitted that I didn't trust her. On top of everything else, I noticed a few days before she went though my Facebook account as I slept. I wrote it off as us being even since I had gone through her phone before. Besides, the only thing I had to hide from her was the lengths I went to see through her lies.

Within 30 minutes, I left. I had this feeling that we were broken up, even if neither one of us said it. One of the questions brought up in our discussion that night was, "How do we get passed this?" I wasn't sure if we would. Months later, having access to all the texts I am now posting, she didn't think so either. Moments after I left, she invited White Trash Looking Actor over and it seems the next day she was supposed to break-up with me... and, clearly, there was more going on between them than she was ever going to admit.

No Service   **5:43 PM**

Messages   **White Trash Looking Actor**   **Edit**

Aug 17, 2009 8:09 PM

I'm really glad you called. I know I must like you alot because you make me feel happy. You know? The kind of happy that comforts me, with reassurance that I'm not alone in the world and that all hope isn't lost. I haven't felt this in a long time. :)

— White Trash Looking Actor ←

Aug 18, 2009 5:44 PM

Thank u so much for coming over! I had a really great time with u. Without ur support I'd be a complete mess right now. I greatly appreciate all that u do for me. And no need to apologize for being sensitive. I would be too. I don't see u any differently at all... I could have easily picked that up instead of what I got so I'd be a hypocrite if I judged u. It's hard to have that talk and I appreciate ur honesty. I have a lot of respect for u! I'll def call u later. Tks again for being there for me. Mwuah!

Hades I feel the exact same way Can i call u?

Aug 18, 2009 4:32 PM

Hey, thanks for letting me hang at yo' place. Sorry about getting so self conscious about sharing that info with you. I'd never had to 'have that talk' before. Thanks for being cool about it. So, call me later after you talk with Chris. I want you to feel as comfortable as you can with me, and I understand how difficult it can be to let go of certain security blankets. So for what it's worth, I'm 100% willing to be that guy for you, if you need it. Xoxo. :)

Aug 18, 2009 10:40 PM

Are you home? Can I come over and buy a xanex from you?

www.lifewithhades.com   **Send**

- 143 -

CHAPTER 46
This Ends Here... Maybe?

The ear on the wall incident gave us both a lot of stuff to think about, and the next evening when we talked about it, we both decided it was time for some space. We were both unhealthy individuals that somehow wound up together and "for better or worse" had somehow become "for bad or worse." We should have broken up this night, spent time apart, and eventually moved on. Maybe remain friends, occasional acquaintances, maybe not. But, that's what we should have done.

Instead, we took some time, but continued to text, talk and at times see each other. One thing was for sure, for our own reasons, neither one of us was ready for it to be over. The drama and adrenaline were too addicting, at least it was for me, anyway. There were a few occasions that I wrote up my feelings and every time the letters ended with, "We don't belong together." Of course, I always deleted that part before sharing my feelings with Hades.

Even during this time of trial separation, I tried to make sacrifices for her: I made myself available, I fixed problems she was having, even went as far as when her computer was too slow for her to work on, took RAM out of my own computer to salvage hers. The never ending cycle was, just that, never ending: the more I gave, the more she took; the more she took, the more I gave.

One Sunday afternoon I went over to her place after seeing a friend, and actually spending time outside, especially before sunset, I realized just how depressing her place was. It was always dark, the drapes always closed, lights on in the middle of the day, and always a complete mess. The bedroom I cleaned was again cluttered, the smell of poop pungent in the air. Had I had enough? She couldn't not lie and that was evident. I remember storming out of there telling her to, "just figure it out." Nothing more, nothing less. It seemed simple enough, if you want to be with someone, be with them or if you want to act single, then be single. A security blanket is there to be laid in, not walked on.

I had no proof, but I figured Hades was, in fact, cheating on me with at least one guy, if not multiple men. As I left that day, I felt a bit relieved, a weight somewhat lifted off my chest. As the sun bathed me in its warmth, I felt like Superman.

I wasn't going to stand there and be mistreated... not forever, anyway.

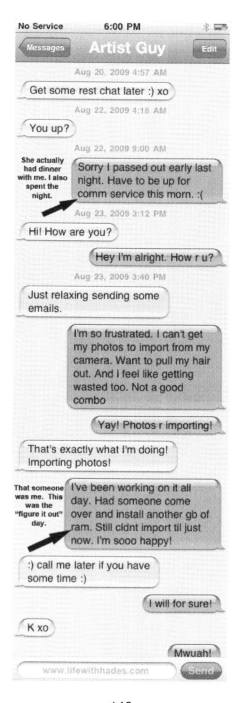

CHAPTER 47
Quitters Never Win, Winners Never Quit

I was about ready to call it. Hades was no longer the girl that I loved. The woman that I laughed with, participated in crazy videos, and the one I took to a Harlem Globetrotters game seemed non-existent. Even now, as we spent most nights apart, the dramatic parts were even fading. The adrenaline was being replaced with sadness.

I woke up in Hades' bed for what I thought might be the last time. I attempted to be physical and when she pulled away, I knew it was over. I don't remember drinking the night before, but something happened when I got up. Maybe I got up too fast, but I felt extremely dizzy once I got on my feet.

I told her, she didn't offer much consoling, so I left to go home, shower, and go to work. As the day passed, the dizziness faded, but it was replaced with nausea and a headache. Hades sent me a text to check in. I gave her a short update and left it at that. I didn't want to trouble her or make her feel like she had to come take care of me. I'm independent and am fully capable of taking care of myself.

Almost nine and a half hours later, she checked back in. By this time the headache became a migraine and I was finally getting home from work. Again, I didn't insist or even ask her to do anything, she said she wanted to bring me medication, but was busy hanging with White Trash Looking Actor. If I didn't think it was over before, I knew it was now.

She said she'd bring me NyQuil and as I laid in bed for two hours waiting for her to show, she finally walked through the door. She poured me a dose and as I downed it, she told me she had to leave, that her roommate was locked out. In and out in 10 minutes. I was not just sad but disappointed. As my head throbbed and she walked out the door, I thought about the seizures, Las Vegas, strep throat, and the week long hospital stay from an ulcer. It wasn't just rude and unfair for her to leave, it was simply mean.

She told me she'd go home and come right back. And for the next 5 hours I received calls and texts with every excuse as to why she wasn't back yet. She used the roommate excuse too many times, and I knew she just had somewhere better to be.

She said she went home, let her roommate in, then had to talk to her Female Musician Friend who just got dumped. On her way back she claimed that she forgot to get her dog and had to turn around as well as was stuck in a police check-point. In reality, she asked her Female Musician Friend to meet her for a drink in Silverlake, then went home, grabbed her dog, and finally came back.... at 3:30 AM.

I was awake the entire time and in between throwing up and a throbbing headache, I was making bets if she was actually going to ever make it back. When she finally did arrive, about 15 minutes later I dozed off.

At around 9am, I woke up, Hades was nowhere to be seen. I found her sleeping in the hallway, her laptop on its side, sitting in a puddle of melted pistachio ice-cream. I stepped over and went into the bathroom, her phone sat there charging on the counter. All the answers I wanted were there. All I had to do was lock the door and look.

I didn't. Instead, I washed my hands, both literally and figuratively. I went back out, picked up the computer and took it into the kitchen to clean it off. By that time, Hades awoke, asked me how I was feeling and then crawled into my bed.

As she slept, I pulled out the boxes I originally bought to move into her place and began packing all her stuff into them. Around 11am, I went to her, tapped her awake and told her I had to go to work. She asked if she could sleep a few more hours.

"That's not a good idea," I said.

"Huh?" she asked as sat up.

"I think we're done."

She looked around, not sure what to do. "Okay," s said with little emotion, "I need to get my things."

"Everything is right there."

She tried to argue, I wouldn't have it. I offered to help carry her belongings down, but she refused. The moment the door closed behind her, I broke down.

Timeline as it really happened that day:

Hades began her juggling act by texting both White Trash Looking Actor and me at 10:28 AM. While I told her how sick I was, she was making plans to visit him on set later that evening.

12 hours later she loaded me up with NyQuil and left saying Roommate was locked out, when in reality she was meeting her Female Musician Friend for a drink. All while I was suffering a migraine.

At the same time she was texting Roommate and telling him to ignore me if I tried to contact him. She had to cover her ass.

Five hours later she finally came back and fell asleep in my hallway. I honestly have no idea how she lives her life each day with so many tracks to cover and so many lies to remember.

That's the best I can do to summarize it all here, which does it a disservice. Unfortunately, it just won't all fit in the book. However, if you want to see the actual texts and see just how deep the rabbit hole went in these 24 hours, visit:

TheRabbitHole.info

CHAPTER 48
You're Pathological

I not only broke up with her but I also threw her ass out. It was pretty bad even looking at it from my side of things, but she deserved it. She wanted to pretend she was single, so I was making it so she didn't have to pretend anymore. Of course, she would probably blindly attempt to get into a deeper relationship with White Trash Looking Actor, which was something I don't think he wanted. Maybe he wanted her when she wasn't technically available, but now that I did what she couldn't do, by ending us, she was now free and clear to be in a relationship with him.

It still drove me nuts that I didn't have the whole story, and I was on the verge of emailing White Trash Actor Guy and just telling him, "she's all yours," because I assumed that he didn't know I existed either. I figured if she was playing him as much as she was playing me, then I could throw a wrench in two of her relationships at one time. However, I didn't do anything.

Hades: again. I wish I had spared u the pain of ever knowing me because I'm not worth it. I can't believe I made u feel so horrible about yourself. It's unforgiveable and I have never felt so ashamed or low.

Aug 28, 2009 2:02 PM

Me: There is nothing good or wonderful about me. Can you please answer one thing honestly. It would mean a lot to me just to know. Did you ever cheat on me?

No. But I did make myself seem single for attention when Id feel bad about myself. And so I did hang out with guys under that assumption.

You never even just kissed any of them to keep that assumption alive?

I did kiss someone.

Who? When?

Artist Guy: I don't know exactly when but probably around late may.

It was the day I threw her out, that she finally admitted to actually kissing Artist guy. Of course, if I hadn't been so hurt and blinded by thoughts that I just lost my "soulmate," I would have realized just how sick and twisted Hades really was. This kissing incident was something she denied, and if you recall, swore on her dead brother's name that it never went as far as it actually did.

Our texts went back and forth all day, me telling her how I was done putting up with lying, her apologizing and telling me just how "fucked up in the head" she really is. Our texts were finally hitting 10 at a time, so eventually later that night we did what we shouldn't have done, and saw each other. We were obviously going to talk, and she mumbled too much to do it by phone.

I told her I wanted to be in her life, but I couldn't if this is how she was going to do things. I told her she needed to get therapy, and she agreed. Earlier in the day I called her a Pathological Liar, which really offended her more than anything. She argued she was not Pathological, and again used the defense that it was her mother that brought her up this way... to lie to keep the peace.

So now I was getting definitions read to me explaining the difference between liars, both Pathological and Compulsive. For some reason, being a Compulsive Liar she was okay with, because it meant the lying was by choice instead of something built in her. And if she wasn't broken from the start, she had some kind of ability to redeem herself someday. Honestly, if it's a choice, it seems much more worse, but either way, lying is lying.

We continued to talk. We continued to text. She took me up on my offer to pay for her therapy, which I was happy to do if it meant she might fix this problem. She also told me over and over how she screwed up really bad, while she continued to do what she did best: playing on my sympathies while also playing the field.

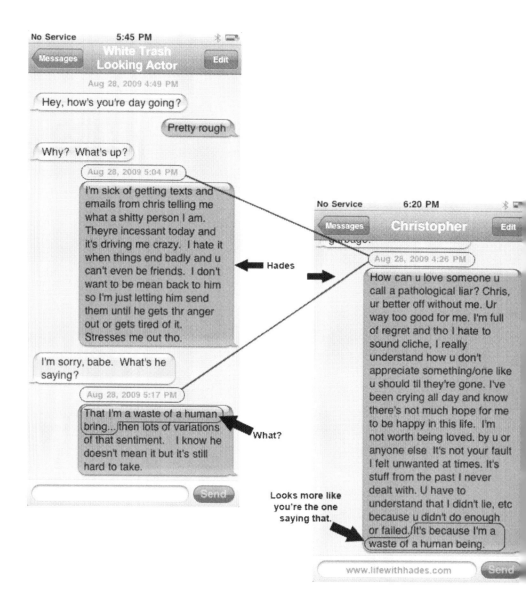

Christopher...

Aug 28, 2009 2:16 PM

> I'm sorry. I feel like shit

Thanks for telling me. I guess you won't have to pretend anymore. I guess there is a trade off to that though. Why did you even want to marry me?

Aug 28, 2009 2:30 PM

> I really did want to marry u. I felt like when I was with u I didn't go to that destructive side. And I liked that- i never thought that was a possibility for me caise thats how ive always been and i really wanted a life with u. We had so much fun and u r unlike any other person I've ever met. I truly do love u. But iVe never dealt with that dark side of me. The kiss with didn't mean anything except it made me feel better and wanted at the time. I have a real problem with that. There's something inside me that's just empty and it's pathetic I do things like that to feel better about myself.

CHAPTER 49
Hop On In, I'll Get Ya There

As our relationship broke down, so did my car. One flat turned into two and I decided that since I was starting anew, that I would get a new car. I didn't want to put any money into the old car, and since I lived about a mile from work, I would just go car-less until I had a new set of wheels. A few days into this I mentioned it to Hades, and remembering how much I drove her around after she totaled her car, I guess she felt like she owed me at least one ride. She offered to pick me up the next morning and take me to work.

I was leery to this. I did want to see her, spend a little time together, but I knew she would probably be 30 minutes late if she showed up at all. Odds were she'd go to bed around 6am and sleep all day, text me around 4pm apologizing for no showing. I did want to see her, so I accepted the offer. We hung up the phone and I went to bed.

At 5am, I awoke to my phone ringing. As expected, Hades was still awake. I answered the phone and immediately heard tone... not a dial tone, but a huff in her voice that was all too familiar.

In my life, I have an ex who has become like a sister. It was this friend that Hades had a problem with at my company's party. It was this friend that unfriended Hades immediately on Facebook when we broke up. It was just before 5am this morning that Hades noticed that and wanted to discuss it. I have no control over my friends, ex or not, or what they do. These two had an issue and it wasn't about jealousy, it was my friend saw through Hades' facade. My friend is an Italian and has mob-like loyalty and was happy to cut ties as soon as I did.

But at 5am, Hades wanted answers. Answers I couldn't give her. When I was boxing up Hades' belongings, ready to throw her out, I only assumed she and her friends would probably de-friend me. Once Hades was single, I figured she would relish in it. She did immediately take our relationship down, but none of her friends reacted. In time, I thought, they would.

Our conversation would have carried on until the time Hades was to pick me up if her phone didn't die. So a three hour conversation was cut to 45 minutes. As soon as her battery held enough charge the texts came through. Eventually she just dropped it and said she'd see me in a couple hours.

I went back to sleep, woke up at my normal time, and although I had been going into work earlier, I told Hades to pick me up at 10am. At 10:04am, as I stood outside, she texted that she was stuck in traffic. All in she was no more than 15 minutes late, which was rather surprising. Maybe she was trying to change her ways for the better.

As she approached the mid-mark to my office, I asked if she'd like to go get coffee. She agreed. We had a nice talk. She told me all about how the day before she went to the beach alone to reflect on herself, us, and the bad decisions she's made in the past. She told me the solitude gave her some new insight on herself and how she wanted to not just be a better person but how she could restore my faith and trust in her.

These were all things I needed to hear. Of course, they were all lies. She did go to the beach, but not alone. Artist Guy was with her.

CHAPTER 50
Lying on the Beach

Had I known then what I know now, Hades would have been just a memory, some good but enough bad. However, she continued to tell me exactly what I wanted to hear. I thought she was actually putting effort into redeeming all the mistakes she made. On Labor Day we decided to pack the dogs into the new car and venture out to Huntington Beach. It's one of the few places that allow dogs.

Overall, it was a good day, until the sun started to set, and Hades' slowly turned into the monster that she is. All of a sudden I was being grilled by questions that really didn't matter. Mostly, what my friends knew of our situation. That fact remained that Hades lied to me, was caught several times over, and when I finally did break up with her, I did tell my friends the gist of why. Now she was shutting down, as her mistakes were now apparently my cross to bear. She kept saying that now if we got back together, my friends would never forgive her. And looking back, they shouldn't.

As day turned to night, we finally packed up the car and headed home, which is when she asked to know what friends knew what about her. I happily told her, because, they were her mistakes and should be her regrets. Afterward she shut down and since the therapist she was supposed to go to that week was a referral from mine, she was ready to back out. One thing was for certain, if she missed her therapy appointment, I would know then she wasn't ready to make amends.

She was in Huntington Beach with me. Nowhere near Santa Baraba

After about three missed exits and an extra 30 minutes driving and talking, we finally made it home. I expected her to ask me to leave, but she didn't. We went up to her messy condo where I found her sitting on the bathroom floor bawling. Looking back, crocodile tears were one of Hades' many weapons and I was a sucker for it.

I told her that if we could get though this hurdle, we could get though anything. All I wanted was to continue to see her change for the better and for her to know what how committed I was to this... and I was about to show her just how serious I was.

CHAPTER 51
Date Night

I broke up with her. I thought she was trying to win me back, but now know that was hardly the case at all. Yet, in the moment, I wanted her to feel loved and cherished, and all she had to do in return was give back the same. Simple, right? I thought so.

We planned a date night. I made a reservation and knowing she would be late told her it was an hour earlier than it was. I arrived on time to pick her up and looked around the house, which was straightened up a bit, albeit still a bit in shambles, but the girl was definitely trying. With the 60 minute leeway, we arrived to dinner on time. A little hidden away restaurant on Laurel Canyon. I didn't want to valet tonight, so we parked down the street. Hades jokingly complained.

The meal was good, we had been here together before. It was a romantic place, plenty of candle light, small yet not crammed, and wonderful mussels, which we ordered for an appetizer.

Conversation was nice, Hades looked great, and we occasionally touched each other's hand.

Half way through our bottle of wine, Hades turned serious, voicing how she was scared to see me, afraid I would leave her again. Her concerns were valid; I did throw her out, an action that was also valid. I told her, as things turned deep, as this is not how I thought this night would go. You see, after dog beach, during the conversation on the way home, I had made a decision, one that Hades would refer to as "on the fly."

I'm not one for spontaneity. I'm actually quite predictable most of the time. If something seems like it's on a whim, it's most likely been thought out before. This week, I took a trip to a jewelry store and picked out a ring. Yes, an engagement ring. Nothing boisterous, but a good ring and replaceable when the time was right.

The heavy conversation came to an end, we finished dinner, and walked to the car. The reason I didn't valet is because this was the moment I was waiting for all night. I was afraid the ring box was going to be noticeable in my pocket, but she had no idea what was about to happen.

As usual, I opened her car door and she sat down. I got lower to put the bag from the restaurant in the car near her feet. It was at this moment I went from crouching down to one knee. I presented the box, opening it during the reveal. I don't even remember what I said, but I knew Hades would, in pure Borderline fashion, be really excited or very turned off. That's when I heard, "Yes. Yes. Yes, yes, yes, yes, YES!!"

We went from being broken-up to engaged just like that. Glowing, Hades immediately had to call her mom and tell her the good news. She tried to explain how we went from 0 to 80 just like that, but I don't think her parents quite understood. Hades hung up the phone and excused herself to pee just outside the car. Yes, she couldn't hold her excitement or urine in, so she squatted down and peed right there just off the sidewalk.

It was much later I realized Lord of the Rings was wrong. The epic story told me how a ring could change a person. I hoped this ring, would not just form a union, but would vex out all the bad traits Hades had within. Unfortunately, she was a Gollum long before I came along.

CHAPTER 52
E=mc²

Hades was to do a writing session with her Best Guy Friend, which was the first day post engagement that Hades wanted to spend with someone else. It was a Saturday afternoon that they were supposed to get together. This, of course, brought back flooding feelings of insecurity, things I didn't want to feel anymore. But, I could either trust that her "Yes!" to my proposal meant she would change her ways or I could continue living in mental Hell.

Later that night she called to see what I was doing and told me they scrapped the writing idea to go record music and Best Guy Friend's cousin's house. She invited me over. Her speech was slurred and I assumed these two would definitely be drinking together. I wasn't really prepared for the next part, when she said, "...and I may have done some E."

That took me off guard. I had never experimented with E before, but I knew the basics. The idea of her with two guys, tripping out on E was not exactly heart warming. Best Guy Friend was in a serious relationship, one of which I would know more about later this night, so I wasn't worried about anything happening.

I finished what I was doing and headed over there. Although Hades was high, it was nice to hear her keep referring to me as her fiance. Soon after I got there, Best Guy Friend took a call from his girlfriend and in the corner I could tell he was getting scolded for being with Hades. I understood being on both ends of that call and felt for the guy. His girlfriend did not like Hades and this would come out more and more after this night. His cousin, a music producer, just wanted to lay tracks.

Hades wanted to be a singer, but that was another thing she self-sabotaged. Her voice was fine, but she always said she couldn't carry a tune, so every time she got up to the microphone, her insecurities kicked in, and she just lowly talked. If anything, I thought it was cute.

Eventually, Hades pulled me aside and put a tablet into my hand. I figured the G didn't do anything to me, so what the hell. I figured, if anything, I would just get sick. The worst part was when she said to chew it.

Whether or not I was going to feel anything, I was unprepared for, so I quickly got Hades out of there and drove her home. The entire drive, I didn't feel a thing. Hades kept repeating to me, "I'm gonna take care of you." It was the first time in 9 months that she ever said those words to me.

As we pulled into the garage, I could feel the E kicking in and we went upstairs. I have to say that it is rather amazing. The drug opened up parts of my brain I didn't know existed. I had fallen down the rabbit hole and loved every second of it. I see how people get addicted to it.

Hades decided, in the brink of my euphoria, to tell me that she didn't like the engagement ring I chose for her. It didn't matter at this point, nothing mattered as the Serotonin, Dopamine, or whatever in my brain was exploding. We would later take the ring back and she chose a new one that did suit her much better. It wasn't even close to the $42,000 ring she liked at Tiffany's, but was very pretty.

That night was remarkable. What was even more incredible was when Hades continued to tell me that she was going to take care of me. Not hearing or feeling that, you sometimes forget about yourself, or at least I did. This relationship had progressed into me taking care of her illnesses, ulcers, seizures. The one time I needed her when I was sick, she was completely absent and left me alone.

Now, for the first time, here she was, offering herself to me. I was allowed to let go and here she was ready to catch me. Sadly, the only way Hades can care about someone is if it's drug-induced sympathy.

CHAPTER 53
Four Word Question; One Word Answer

One question. One answer. That's all it took and immediately it felt like all the problems were gone. I didn't expect them to just disappear, but I did expect them to be worked on in and out of therapy. That was something we both agreed on, but for the moment everything was once again "happy."

We both started to tell the word and not too soon as I had to go to Arizona again to spread my Grandfather's ashes. Hades agreed to go. I told my mom before we arrived about the proposal, she was happy. We waited to be with other family members to tell them. Our engagement wasn't the reason we were there, so we didn't make much of an announcement.

I think my family was happy and liked Hades. Hades was open about her addiction past, so I think my mom was leery about me marrying her. What was worse was while everyone was up early to spend time with the family, Hades slept in. This was noticed by all but really only mentioned by mom. Specifically, one night we all spent together in the same house and although I tried to get her up, Hades missed breakfast. She finally got up, around noon, only because I told her that everyone was asking about her whereabouts. While everyone else was not only showered and ready, but also cleaning the kitchen or straightening up, Hades came out clad in pajamas. She was directed to the dried out eggs and other scraps of remaining food, much like a dog.

Hades mentioned how insecure she felt for sleeping in, but this never stopped her from doing it again and again, no matter what my family or what anyone really thought of her. Hades, for lack of a better word, was selfish. She was that person that took what she wanted, didn't care what anyone really thought of her, but would continuously try to guilt me into believing she did. If she actually cared about anyone but herself, including my mourning family, she would have gotten out of bed like everyone.

Eventually we departed my family in Phoenix where we stayed at a resort. Before we left to head back to Los Angeles, we spent the day at the pool. There was a lazy river and we just floated around in circles together for hours. The whole time just staring into each others eyes. Hades kept saying the same thing in as many ways as she could, "I can't believe we almost threw this all away." Looking back, I can't believe I allowed it to continue while she would again throw it away.

CHAPTER 54
Two Tired

As the status quo was retained, I once again gave notice to my landlord that I would be moving out. It seemed logical at the time, since by this point my place was a glorified storage unit.

Hades was now, more than ever or would ever be in the future, trying to make me a part of her circle of friends. An old friend of her's, Aspiring Director, was moving back to Los Angeles. This was a guy that recently broke-up with his girlfriend and an old friend of hers. Him and I spoke on the phone but this lunch with the three of us was to be the first time I would meet him. It was nice when males in her life were friends and not always trying to figure out some angle on her; it was these friends she didn't try to hide.

While Hades was heading my way, she somehow managed to blow out both of her front tires. I rushed over to make sure she and her car were okay. We left her car in the parking lot of the Universal Amphitheater and headed to lunch as planned (albeit now a bit late).

During lunch, Aspiring Director mentioned that he was looking for a place to live. Since my place was basically empty for the next month, I offered it to him, no strings attached.

The next couple of days Hades left it up to me to figure out the car situation. The Amphitheater also called me putting a deadline on the removal of the car as well. The problem wasn't just two flat tires, but also the shattered rim. Getting a new rim for a 2002 Volvo isn't the easiest, quickest, or cheapest thing to do, not to mention taking the time to actually get the car moved.

Nothing is ever easy in Hades' world, unless of course you are Hades. For her things seem to magically just happen for you: condos clean themselves, dogs never have to go outside, and cars magically are fixed.

AAA was great at getting the car to Costco as the tires were only a few months old and still under warranty, but the cracked rim was still an issue. I called the dealership and they would have to special order it. Instead, I took a day off work and visited every junkyard in Junkyard Alley in the Valley. Finally, 4 hours and $200 dollars later, I found my rim. It still had a bald tire on it, but it was the right size, shape, year, and color. Victory!

The only job Hades had was to show up to Costco so they could verify the warranty, which I finally managed to get her to do, 5 minutes before they closed. To this day, Hades never asked what all was entailed to make her mobile again. To her defense, I never hinted it was more than a minor set-back, which is what being a partner, at least in my mind, is all about.

CHAPTER 55
Art Show

It's weird looking back and each story I write, I'm that much further away from it all. Some days I wonder what has become of Hades, other days there's certain things I miss, the laughs and inside jokes occasionally creep into my head. Then other days, particularly right now, I remember things that just shouldn't be relived, yet as a storyteller, and someone that learns from history, will do just that.

Hades lived in a three-story condo and from what I could tell, three neighbors stood out. Whacked out neighbor I've discussed, there was also Single Gay Guy across the hall who related to Hades' substance abuse with the many blacked out stories of his own to tell (He told me this was his attempt to reach her). The last was a very bitchy and plump sexagenarian who never left her home without a short skirt, stiletto heels and make-up that must have been applied by Homer's make-up rifle. The Sexagenarian despised Hades and had tried numerous times, as Treasurer of the HOA, to somehow kick Hades out of the complex.

Hades and I had numerous in-depth talks about us, our engagement, and our future together. One thing always stood out among the rest, the verbal dedication to not only be together but our constant devotion that we could get though anything together.

This was one of those nights. Artist Guy was hosting a event and Hades wanted to take me, introduce me to him again for the first time, and show me that, although they did kiss, that it was not only something we could get though but was also not a threat. I agreed to go. This was a test for her, but also for me. Some might see it as just a kiss, and maybe I was over reacting to it, but it was a kiss that happened while Hades and I were dating and committed, therefore a risk.

We attended the show, I drank enough to numb my nerves while Hades drank enough to numb her inhibitions. The night seemed to go fine, I spoke to Artist Guy, I forgave the past, and was ready to move on. We left the party on an enlightened path and that's when either the alcoholism or the Borderline personality kicked in and a fight was brewing.

Honestly, I don't even remember now what started it all. Hades was hungry so we cruised through the Taco Bell drive-thru and as we walked toward her place, she said something that just struck a nerve. I said something back and she stopped dead in her tracks in front of Sexagenarian's door and just slammed her large soda as hard as she could toward the ground. Pepsi flew everywhere and then my drink quickly followed.

What happened next was probably our biggest argument up to this day. Doors slammed, voices were raised, and what was to be a big moment of getting past some of our past, was ruined. At some point Sexagenarian woke up and started yelling about the soda, the carpet, the wall and whatever lurked behind the two inches of make-up was not happy.

I talked to Sexagenarian and explained the mess was an accident and would be professionally cleaned and afterwards I went back inside the condo. This fight was stupid and I was ready to end it dramatically... with four shots of Vodka back-to-back. On that note, I laid down, and on another note, I got back up to throw up for a good 10 minutes.

Eventually Hades came to my aid, after I woke her up on the couch to tell her how violently ill I had become. We blacked out soon after that.

The next morning I had to re-apologize to the Sexagenarian and another neighbor for the corn syrup laden accident and agreed to have the carpet cleaned. That would turn into another couple hundred dollar charge and in the late morning, when all the neighbors were calmed, Hades and I apologized to each other for our actions, thus continuing the vicious circle that would be our relationship. On the bright side, my life is now Vodka free!

CHAPTER 56
If You Lived Here, You'd Be Home Right Now

Moving day was set for the last weekend of October. I had to have my apartment vacated on Halloween, which fell on a Saturday this year. I had a normal amount of furniture and enough stuff to box up that it would take at least a day to handle it. Hades was very vocal about helping me. As always things would change, but here was the plan in it's simplest form:

The Thursday before Hades was to pick up her East Coast Girlfriend from the airport at noon and the two of them would meet me at my place. The three of us would then pack the boxes. Friday the movers would come and take everything and we would be done. Saturday would be there was anything left to do, but since it was Halloween, I not only hoped but planned for a free day.

I woke up Thursday and headed into the office for the morning and planned on seeing my fiancee and her friend at 1pm. At 11:30am there was no work from Hades. At noon still no word. Finally around 12:15pm, 15 minutes after her friend landed, she called me and said she just woke up. It was time to once again save her day. I told Hades I would go get her friend from the airport and we would meet her at my place.

I rushed to LAX and swooped up East Coast Girlfriend, finally meeting her for the first time. From the initial contact she seemed good. There was a bit of a drug history between her and Hades, but from what I could tell, East Coast Girlfriend was now clean and felt like a good influence on Hades.

ECGF and I arrived, as scheduled, at my place at 1pm. We got to know each other as we packed up dishes and my other belongings. Hades eventually arrived close to 4pm (she made a few personal stops on the way). This was the first time Hades and ECGF had seen each other sometime so while they caught up a bit, I ran out to get some additional boxes. When I returned, Hades was sitting in front of a mirror putting make-up on. By this point, it was close to 5:30pm and she had yet to help me pack one item.

In the weeks prior, Hades decided she wanted to open her own photo studio so had been contacting people about buying a studio. She had her eye on one and I even said I could probably pledge close to 25% of the initial overhead if she could raise the rest. So, we left early on Thursday, barely making a dent on the packing, in order to show ECGF the studio she wanted to buy.

On Friday I met the movers and eventually Hades came over and while I tried explain to her that I could not do this all by myself, she continued to excuse herself to field phone calls about the studio. I was clearly alone on this one. I furiously tried to pack as the large pieces of furniture disappeared while Hades kept doing the same. With each hour, the movers were becoming more expensive so when it appeared that all the big stuff was on the truck, I decided that I would use the free day to do the odds and ends.

Halloween morning, I woke up before Hades and told ECGF I was heading over to my place to finish up. She asked if I needed help and I wasn't about to allow her to do even that much more work than Hades, so I politely declined. I drove the 25 minutes to my place and loaded up the first load and came into to find Hades, showered, dressed and ready to help... No wait, I didn't find that at all, what I found was Hades was still sleeping.

I made several attempts to wake her and she did finally rise. Instead of offering to help, she grabbed some pizza from the night before, went to the couch, and joined ECGF for some TV and computer time. I told her I was going to go back to my place and attempt to get it cleaned out. This is when I assumed she'd offer to help, but Hades made no move to leave that couch. So I left.

Packing took me the rest of the day. At no time did Hades even check in. Even with all the other problems and issues we had, this one was a pretty tough pill to swallow. I really was in this alone. I was the problem solver while my partner was an absentee ballot. It was a depressingly sad moment as I sat there in the middle of a near empty apartment that was only mine for six more hours.

As I texted Hades at 6pm telling her I was nearly done, she replied asking if I could get a bottle of wine on my way home. I chuckled to myself as I looked at my car and how I used every inch of space to avoid having to come back. I literally did not have room for even a bottle of wine. I had to go home first.

Exhausted and tired, I couldn't hide the disappointment on my face. She complained that she did offer to help, which was true to the point that upon leaving for my second trip, I forgot something so ran back upstairs. At which point, sitting on the couch, in her pajamas, laptop open, pizza on her side, glasses on, she asked if I wanted her to come. It was in that moment that in my head I said, "Yes, I would like that very much," but then that played out with her finishing what she was doing, getting dressed, finding three side projects to do, and us finally getting there 2 hours later. At this point, it just didn't make sense. So, I said, "No, it's fine."

I told her that she never has to ask me for help. I just help. I fix things and sometimes I'd like the same in return.

CHAPTER 57
For Medicinal Purposes Only

Up to this point, medically speaking, Hades was pretty intense. She had two seizures, a "fall" from a balcony, strep throat, and a bleeding ulcer. She owed money to Cedar Sinai, Burbank Hospital, Sunrise Hospital in Las Vegas, Centennial Hospital also in Vegas, not to mention the Vegas Urgent Care as well as two ambulance companies. All these bills were generated over the course of four months.

By the sight of the stack of unopened medical bills sitting on the counter, Hades clearly did not want to deal with the thousands of dollars of debt. I told her many times over that we needed to start talking to the hospitals in order to keep her out of collection. What I was beginning to understand is when I said "we" ultimately she heard "me." Finally, I took four hours one day to open, organize, figure out what she owed, and match the services up with the insurance claims. Then I systematically started calling each vendor attempting to not only renegotiate the debt but also put Hades on payment plans. Of course, Hades was still unemployed therefore her payment plans ultimately were now my payment plans.

After that, she didn't even notice that the collection phone calls she'd receive daily all but stopped. I told her I spoke to every single one and after that she never asked about it again. I don't think it was until after I moved out that she realized just how much I took care of her. I left with her a yellow file folder that contained all her medical bills organized with dates of when each partial payment was due. I can only assume all that work was for nothing as each one immediately slipped into the "never to be paid" category.

CHAPTER 58
I'm Ready For My Close-Up

Hades had appeared in a handful of music videos, always appearing in some form of bra/panty combo. They were typical low-budget bands with typical low-budget shoots. One story she told me about one of the videos of the past, she shot it the desert and was high on GHB the entire time. Between takes her ex-boyfriend would load her up so she could get through the day.

During this time a friend of mine was casting a video for a group filled with not just well known members, but also successful and highly regarded musicians. Although the budget was the same; the talent itself was not. When I sold them on her for the lead, she just elevated herself a notch.

One thing that remained a constant was her competitive need to outshine both FFPRMF and Once Famous Video Vixen. Once Famous' fame was 80's fame, when music videos meant something, so Hades was not about to one up her, but FFPRMF was another story. Hades shot the video, and although it only paid her a couple hundred dollars, it was the YouTube exposure she was after.

Quickly the hits rose and she was soon to have more views than FFPRMF's highest clicked video. Hades was proud and even more excited that the producers of the video wanted her back for another. She saw another couple hundred bucks but more importantly: more exposure.

Of course, things quickly changed and while packing my apartment with Hades and East Coast Girlfriend, I received an email that the video was completely changed and they no longer needed her. The producer explained that the concept changed from needing one girl to using at least 6-12 in a pseudo montage. This meant they couldn't pay all the girls so they decided to just use friends, etc. that would show up and do it for free. I told him this was important to her and if she could still be involved and considered the "star," I would happily cover the $250.

I explained to Hades the changed video, that she was still the "star" and was the only one getting paid. She was a little disappointed but what made it all okay was that since East Coast Girlfriend also had some tattoos, that she too could be involved.

But, as always, nothing was ever that easy...

CHAPTER 59
Shattered: Literally and Figuratively

The second music video was scheduled. Instead of Hades being the only female, she was now going to be lumped into a montage of about 8 other women, but was still being told that she would be the most featured female. Also, I agreed to with the producers to pay her out of my pocket so she could still think nothing else had changed. East Coast Girlfriend was still in town and since other women were being cast, it was agreed that she could be in Hades' parts of the video.

I left work to pick the girls up and attempted to get them there on time. Hades' now had this starlet attitude since getting asked back for the second video. "I'm the client, we can get there whenever we want," was her general attitude toward this project. If only she knew they dropped her from the video just days earlier. I had to correct her and tell her that they were actually the client in this scenario. We arrived 45 minutes.

Hades and East Coast Girlfriend shot their portion which was more or less just making gestures to the camera. The overall theme of the video, without getting too specific, was a montage of girls posing for the camera. Pretty simple and Hades and East Coast Girlfriend did exactly what they were supposed to do. On the way out, Hades lingered in the stairwell a few moments trying to eavesdrop on what the Producers thought of the day. I was a mere couple feet away and heard nothing, but that's not how Hades would remember it.

As the sun was setting the three of us drove to dinner and this was when Hades started shutting down and her Borderline Personality was taking over. If the transformation was a visual one, I would picture Venom taking over Spider-Man's body. The good parts of her now buried as the vile poison was ready to be unleashed. Hades said she heard the Producers either mock or insult the shoot. Again, I was a few steps below Hades and heard nothing of the sort. Hades went quiet.

East Coast Girlfriend and I exchanged glances and a few words as Hades excused herself from the table. It was clear that ECGF wasn't fond of the personality change either. It was at this point that Hades then would start recalling other things about me that annoyed her and ask for some kind of response. At this point, with ECGF right there, I called Hades out. I told her that whenever she was upset by something else, that was the time she unleashed all her insecurities and lashed out. The discussion was quickly becoming a fight.

We ended dinner early and drove home. Hades was inconsolable and I was finally learning that although my nature was to talk through an argument, it was best to leave Hades be until her version of Venom was torn off. Hades used this time to call up Once Famous Video Vixen (aka her Drug Dealer).

It was about this time Hades caught on to the fact that Vixen's five minute visits were odd and most likely obvious of her drug purchases. Therefore, the Vixen would find some excuse to swing by (bring a piece of clothing Hades wanted to borrow, show her some of the jewelry she was selling, etc.). At some point in her quick pop-in, Vixen would ask to use the restroom, which is when she would stash the drugs.

After Vixen left, I decided to go against my better judgment and headed into the bedroom to discuss the things we had been arguing about. At some point, I said something along the lines of, "I don't know what you want to hear." Hades then elevated the fight and said that I was just telling her what she wanted to hear, which was just a form of lying, and therefore the lies she told in the past were equal to what I was doing now. It went above and beyond any form of logic or reason.

I remember laying in bed frustrated and now we were focused on all the lies she told me over our relationship, one of which just came out two days prior. I looked over at a wine glass that was sitting on the desk and envisioned smashing it against the wall. It was at this point I should have walk away. But then she said something that brought up all the resentment I had been holding inside. What it related to was that she was just going to start lying to me again. I told her I would never have that in my life ever again, and I did what I imagined: I smashed that glass.

Unfortunately, at some point in the few minutes prior she picked it up, which meant she was holding it when it went flying through the air. It ended up cutting both our hands. She was bleeding; I was bleeding. The thin wine glass shattered into hundreds, if not thousand of pieces.

I had reached my boiling point and this was the most aggressive I had ever become toward another human being.

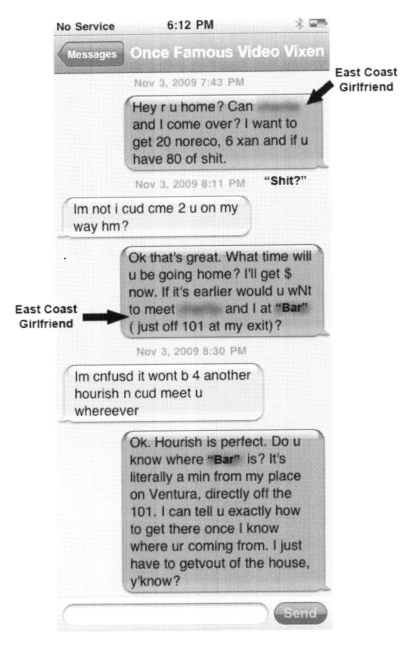

CHAPTER 60
Blood On My Hands

The glass was shattered and although both our hands were bleeding, the blood was all on my hands. I moved in just days ago and now the argument shifted once again to me moving out. Resentment is a huge thing and I suppressed mine so long that it exploded into this. This was a moment I was never going to live down and, again, would have been a good time for us to part ways. However, we didn't and after 24 hours all may have been forgiven but would never be forgotten.

Those 24 hours were very rocky. A few days later when we erupted into another fight, all she would say, after drinking too much were things like:

"Go ahead and hit me, I know you want to!"
"Maybe if you just hit me, you'll finally forgive me for everything I've done."
"Clearly, your only intention of breaking that glass was to hurt me."

This went on all night until I finally told her, "I'm not going to hit you, but if you think unleashing on you will help me, I'll do it verbally." So we sat down and I told her everything:

-All the lies I knew about.
-The times I knew she wasn't home because I came over unannounced.
-How much credibility she lost by swearing on her dead brother's name only to tell me more lies.
-The times trying to figure out where she was by driving all over town.
-The sleepless nights wondering if her MIA actions were just cheating on me.
-All the things that didn't add up, still didn't add up, and never would add up as long as she wasn't going to explain them.

Out of all that, and instead of just addressing the issues at hand, she just labeled me a stalker and I realized she would forever do whatever she wanted and anything I did she would just use against me. She lied to me so many times and was caught every time, she desperately wanted to somehow turn me into the bad guy. She now had all the ammo she felt she needed.

CHAPTER 61
And the Band Played On

Hades put that ammo she now had in her back pocket and waited to use it whenever she felt things shifting out of her control. For now, the wedding would continue as planned. We decided that the ceremony would take place in Santa Barbara, so we went up to check out some venues and meet with a wedding planner.

We looked out the Canary Hotel's rooftop pool where another wedding was currently in progress. We ruled the place out because of the basement location for the reception. That's when we went into the restaurant to grab a drink and a bite to eat when Hades noticed one of her rings was gone (not her engagement ring). She said she must have left it downstairs in the bathroom. She asked me to go get it. After I told her I wasn't going into the women's room, I could see the Borderline Personality kick in.

That's the hardest part of dating a Borderline. The quick change that can ruin a day or even an entire weekend. There's no avoiding it and when a Borderline is ready to go into that love/hate zone, there's no way out.

There was no fixing it now and the day was ruined and we still had a 90 minute drive home. The drive was quiet at first, but in usual Borderline fashion, Hades began questioning me on whatever topic at hand to feed her ego. It wasn't just things to make her feel better, but things to make me feel worse. That's when it always turned into an argument.

We arrived home and to avoid fighting further, she went to take a bath. I could hear Sarah McLachlan's "Angel" playing on a loop for the next hour or so. After a short time I went in to check on her.

I walked in to find what looked like a horrific sight. All I could see were her feet and above them was a red heart with the names of all the people she cared about. The red lipstick it was written in, on first glance, looked like it was smeared on the tile in blood. Hades was passed out, her face just above the water. I honestly thought she was dead.

I grabbed her shoulders and shook her awake. She was surprised to see me in such a state of shock that when I realized she wasn't dead, I broke down. She would later say this wasn't a show for dramatics, but who exactly does it mean when you stage a room to look like a suicide attempt?

CHAPTER 62
Pain in the Neck

I was asked to go speak at a Writer's Symposium in Texas for a couple days so I asked Hades to come along. The trip was, for the most part good, the most daunting being the fact that Hades loved to sleep. One day when the guy who put the whole thing together was planning on taking us out to dinner, Hades didn't get up until 4pm.

Shortly after returning to Los Angeles I pulled my neck and was in almost crippling pain. I needed to go to the doctor the next day. Hades, in her defense, attempted to be there for me. She dipped into her stash of pain killers so I could actually move around until the doctor visit. She made me an appointment and then ran off to do a couple hours at an internship. In the meantime, feeling a bit relaxed, I went to pick up our dogs from my friend that was watching them.

Upon returning home, Hades picked me up and we arrived at my doctor on time. This was around the time that Hades was trying to buy the photo studio she had her eye on and spent most of the few waking hours in the day she had on the phone. Doctor visits were no exception and what should have been a simple visit, she made sure to bring her laptop. She was working away almost in a personal limbo as we sat there in the waiting room.

At some point her phone rang and as she answered the phone, she exited the waiting room and disappeared down the hall. She left me and her belongings behind. That's when the Physician's Assistant called my name. Now I should have been able to walk back, but now on top of a wrenched neck, I had an unattended backpack and a her laptop to deal with.

I asked the PA for a moment and went out into the hallway. Hades was no where to be seen. I called out to her and she came back around the corner, some 100 feet away. You see even when Hades was physically there, she wasn't "there." The world around a Borderline, possible Sociopath, does not exist especially outside their line of sight.

CHAPTER 63
INFP

Randomly, in the middle of the night, Hades sent me an email:

Subject: My Personality according to Myers-Briggs

Apparently there are only 5-6% of INFP's in the general population. Do you think I'm like this? I think it's pretty dead-on, whether I like it or not. :) :(:) :(

INFP
creative, smart, idealist, loner, attracted to sad things, disorganized, avoidant, can be overwhelmed by unpleasant feelings, prone to quitting, prone to feelings of loneliness, ambivalent of the rules, solitary, daydreams about people to maintain a sense of closeness, focus on fantasies, acts without planning, low self confidence, emotionally moody, can feel defective, prone to lateness, likes esoteric things, wounded at the core, feels shame, frequently losing things, prone to sadness, prone to dreaming about a rescuer,

disorderly, observer, easily distracted, does not like crowds, can act without thinking, private, can feel uncomfortable around others, familiar with the darkside, hermit, more likely to support marijuana legalization, can sabotage self, likes the rain, sometimes can't control fearful thoughts, prone to crying, prone to regret, attracted to the counter culture, can be submissive, prone to feeling discouraged, frequently second guesses self, not punctual, not always prepared, can feel victimized, prone to confusion, prone to irresponsibility, can be pessimistic.

In a nutshell, this was Hades. What stood out the most in her report was this blurb:

In conflict situations, INFPs place little importance on who is right and who is wrong. They focus on the way that the conflict makes them feel, and indeed don't really care whether or not they're right. They don't want to feel badly.

This really opened up that mystery box that was Hades, especially when we fought. She didn't care if she did wrong, she only cared that she felt bad getting called out. She had little remorse for her wrong-doings. She was decided that she was hard-wired this way and nothing that I said, did, or felt was going to change this.

Hades loved to research her short-comings not as a way to maybe one day work on them, but to excuse them. It was like the time she defended that she wasn't a Pathological Lair, but a Compulsive one, which apparently in her mind is okay. And now she could label herself "wounded at the core" among other things which meant anything she did was somehow, not only explainable, but justified.

CHAPTER 64
Give Thanks

For Thanksgiving Hades and I decided to forego any family tradition and start our own. In the spirit of the holiday, I booked us a couple nights up in Ventura as well as Thanksgiving dinner for two. I really wanted to get up there at check-in on Wednesday so we could enjoy the days that were set aside just for us.

Tuesday night Hades wanted to stay up all night and make music videos and listen to an eclectic array of songs. It was a needed outlet since there was still the animosity from the last two weeks. We ended up breaking out the FlipCam and making some D-grade short. It was fun and since it was now around 11am on Wednesday, Hades crashed on the couch. I took the day instead of driving the hour North to instead edit our little video.

It was a change of plans, but our late night videos/short films were something that started our relationship and it was a nice feeling to revisit those days where I was surviving on an hour or less sleep on any given night.

"We have so much fun together," was a common phrase when Hades and I first started dating and it was true. If nothing else, we had fun, which was one of the things that always made me second guess my gut feelings on so many issues. We had more fun than two people should be allowed and laughed longer and harder than anyone else in the room. "Why would she throw this away?" was the first question I always asked myself to reason against all that I thought may be happening behind my back.

I was looking for an archived email tonight and was awarded in my search by coming across an old love letter I wrote to Hades. One thing I said to her was, "...all these years my heart may have been inside my chest, but the love that was to go along with it is, and always has been, inside of you." That one hit me hard because when I typed those words out, I meant every one of them. How could these two people so in love fall apart?

Our Thanksgiving was, if nothing else, loving and romantic. Unfortunately, most of the rest of the weekend I spent alone. Hades, always a night owl, would have slept through the weekend if I hadn't kept on trying to wake her up. It was this weekend I wondered how we would spent a life together if I slept at night and she slept in the day. I even researched Polyphasic Sleep, and pondered completely altering my sleep pattern in order to actually spend time with the woman that was to be my wife.

I sacrificed many, many nights of sleep to be with her. One of these weekend nights, we waited too late to get dinner and the only place open was McDonald's. It was so late in fact that they were serving breakfast.

CHAPTER 65
HOA

Since I met Hades, she was at risk of losing her house and her mortgage company wasn't even the biggest threat. She hadn't paid an HOA fee for almost a year. Now that this was my home, I was forced to step in after seeing she now had seven lien letters from the HOA and now the mortgage company was starting to wonder where their payments were.

The HOA was not fond of Hades, in fact, the Sexagenarian Neighbor was the Treasurer and hated Hades to the core. I went over the invoices and called up the law firm that was handling all the liens and possible foreclosure and struck a deal. I would make sure the standard amount was paid along with an extra $1,000 until she was caught up. They agreed to the deal and the HOA was off her back and now on mine.

I next called the Mortgage company and qualified her for an extension which postponed her payments, all Hades had to do was sign a letter agreeing to the flexible terms. I told her to expect the letter within 10 days, sign it, mail it back.

I made the HOA payments and hand-delivered them on-time every month until the day I left. The mortgage letter came, went unopened, and the single agreement sheet was never returned. Instead it went on the one foot stack of mail Hades never looked at. The mortgage company then retracted her extension deal and when I reapplied for her she was denied. The bright side was I applied her into a new program that would reduce her payments and in the interim she was not expected to pay anything. That at least bought her some time.

Assess:	$5776.00
Late:	$528.60
Interest:	$411.05
Atty Fees:	$0.00
HOA & Mgmt:	$650.00
Trustee Costs:	$408.50
Trustee:	$795.00
Totals:	$8569.15

CHAPTER 66
Medical, Dental, and Vision

Hades loathed the insurance plan her parents put her on. Being almost 30 and my fiancee, I decided it would be best to ween her off assistance from her Mom and Dad. Her dad was a quiet and reserved man. I met him once and respected him very much. I felt like it was part of the deal to help make Hades independent from her parents, even if it meant she became dependent on me.

I put her on a new and improved insurance plan which allowed her parents to breathe a sigh of relief while letting Hades have a plan she didn't hate. The plan included dental and vision and she admitted she hadn't been to the dentist in over two years. This was an experience I would not soon forget.

As far as medical went, I booked Hades a physical as she would not book one herself. She said she wanted to find a doctor she could trust that she could discuss her history of drug abuse with so that she could get off the Adderall, pain killers, and whatever else she was buying from the Once Famous Video Vixen.

Then I booked us both teeth cleanings. It was like a couples massage but not nearly as romantic or relaxing. It was this day I found out that Hades was terrified of the dentist. The cleaning went okay but when we had to return to fill cavities, she acted like a cat surrounded by dogs made of water. I called ahead to see how getting her Nitrous to help calm her. They told me it would be an extra $100. I told them to go ahead and add it but not to tell her it was any extra and that I would cover it. As I sat in the waiting room, she texted me that she was about to freak out and have a nervous breakdown. I went into the back to try and talk her out of going into shock. I awkwardly sat there and held her hand as the dentist finished the last bits of drilling and filling.

Sometime before this, her Beagle ate both of our glasses. Mine were the first casualty which didn't seem to bother Hades all that much. I was able to reconstruct them, but one of the lenses was missing. Even after telling her how much I would like to find it, I never once saw Hades lift a finger. It was after her glasses were totally trashed that she would ever bring it up, so I scheduled us vision appointments. The day we were to go, she found a mysterious pill in her room. After looking it up, it turned out to be Morphine. During our exam, she told me that she popped the pill on the way to the appointment, which meant her tests, especially the one for peripheral vision all came out funky. She was considered untestable and had to come back at a later time to retake the tests. Until her prescription was able to be verified we picked out and I paid for her frames and eventual lenses.

All of this was on top of the therapist that she said was helping her get through her issues which included commitment, trust and, of course, addiction. Mental coverage was not on the insurance so that

I was paying for out-of-pocket.

CHAPTER 67
Cloudy Days Ahead

It's raining today in Los Angeles. I'm reminded of a Saturday that Hades and I went to look at a near condemned studio space in Culver City. Although Hades' idea of opening her own photo studio was starting to waiver, she still kept the dream alive. We met a friend of hers and the Realtor to look at a building that was clearly not up to code as the water leaked down the stained pillars that barely held up the roof. Hades had big ideas and even bigger plans, but securing any capital beyond what I offered her was not going to come easy or any time soon. I wanted her to succeed but she was trying to compete with not one, but two former employers that were already set up to do exactly what she wanted. On top of that, the guy she was interning for, who started supportive, now was eluding that her ideas were things he had been trying to implement into his studio the past few months. As the rain pounded on the windshield as we drove home, I offered her an option, "Come work with me," I said.

In the weeks past, she had come to the office with me here and there because an itch had developed in her to venture into film production. She was starting to champion a screenplay written by her friend, the Aspiring Director. I told her she should join me daily and learn at least the basics of creative development. There was an empty office next to mine she could claim as her own. She agreed with a heart-warming smile and would later say, "This really feels like where I'm supposed to be."

I liked having Hades at work with me, but it also added a new hurdle in our relationship. She vocalized how much she wanted to be a part of a team and had this idolization of the idea of becoming a "Power Couple." Yet each and every morning I had to fight with her to even get out of bed and even when she did, we would arrive at the office 1-2 hours later than I wanted to. She would randomly decide to take days off and one day in particular it was impossible to wake her up so I let her sleep. Strangely, I didn't hear from her all day so was all the more shocked when I came home at 7pm to find the house dark. I slowly crept into the bedroom and found her still asleep.

I really tried to allow her to blossom professionally and give her all the tools and resources she could ask for. It was fun to watch her get excited when her project would have even the slightest momentum. It was sad when she would later tell me that the only reason I had her come into the office was to control her.

CHAPTER 68
We Need To Talk

Those four words can send shivers up the spine of anyone when spoken by their significant other, however, on this day it wouldn't come from Hades but a colleague of mine. I was told that a Casting Director friend of mine needed to talk to me and it was important. What was eerily odd was that he asked to see me in person. He lived near where Hades and I lived, so after dropping her off after work I ran over to his place.

We sat down in his apartment complex conference room. This was a good guy that knew every actor in town, if not personally then by name. He could spout out lists of any type you asked for in an almost robotic fashion. I asked for his assistance in the weeks prior to help me find Hades some kind of agent. It was this reason he summoned me over.

Knowing every actor in town meant he knew White Trash Looking Actor, and not just by name, but personally. He had even at one time threw out his name for a project I was working on unaware of any connection that I had to him. He told me that during his talk to agents that one of them knew Hades by a certain reputation and referred to her as White Trash Looking Actor's Girl. Things were alluded to and knowing what I knew could only come to the conclusion that there was some weight into what he was telling me.

I thanked him and went home. Hades knew something was wrong immediately and that's when I asked her, "When did you fuck him?" and she went right on the defensive. She denied the allegations and swore on her dead brothers name, my life and our dogs' lives that he, and I quote Hades here, "never put his dick in my pussy."

Soon after that, instead of having a conversation or even fighting about it, she decided to down three maximum strength bars of Xanax and pass out leaving me not only confused and feeling empty but with a head full of unanswered questions.

CHAPTER 69
Superficially Wounded

Hades slept though the night, even it was drug induced. She would later tell me she woke up and downed another three bars of Xanax with a glass of wine to totally knock her self out. My alarm went off as normal and I, like most people in the world, had no choice but to continue on and go to work.

After a few hours I received that text from her which was a blanket suicidal sounding statement. I didn't know what to do and had to ask my assistant if this was a genuine threat. She told me I should go home immediately, which I did.

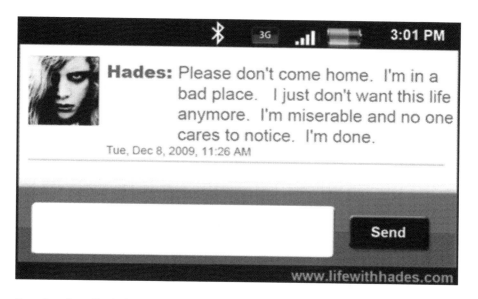

I arrived to find the door latched. Hades barely used the deadbolt let alone the latch. When the latch was on it really only meant she didn't want me to come in. I tried calling her as I did numerous times on the drive home. Like all those times, she didn't answer. The Beagle sat crying at the 4-inch opening almost pleading for me to come in.

I ran down to my car to get tools to open the door and avoid having to kick it down. When I returned to the front door, it was unlocked and left ajar. I slowly walked in to find Hades curled up on the couch in tears, but still in some kind of Xanax hangover. I went over to her and found a steak knife clenched in her fist. I ripped it out of her hand, threw it across the room, and quickly examined her wrists and arms. All I found was a superficial cut across her forearm, which didn't even bleed.

Hades retreated to the bedroom. As she rambled on how I was going to leave her, I felt like the text and the knife was just for show. Maybe it was a cry for help, but I had nothing to give her at the moment. She was labeled as a cheater and an "attempted suicide scene" (not even as dramatic as the one before) wasn't making me change how I felt about the betrayal that she may have done.

Whatever the case, I had to go back to work. When I came home later that night Hades was gone. For hours she offered me nothing more than that she "was safe." This was my punishment for challenging her and calling her out. Instead of acting like an adult about it, she would vanish and send cryptic messages for my scattered thinking to fill in the holes. Later she told me that Once Famous Video Vixen came and picked her up.

She wouldn't come home until the next night and since she was treating our relationship like a game, that's when I offered her a get out of jail free card. I told her I needed to know the truth and if she lied to me now, I would never be able to trust her. And, if she lied to me now, eventually I would find out, and when I did, I would have no choice but to leave her. However, if she was honest, no matter what the answer, we would work through it together. My one and only question was, "Did you sleep with White Trash Looking Actor?"

Her reply was a resounding, "No." She then recited a list of reasons why she would never hook up with him, one of those being his admission to having genital warts.

CHAPTER 70
Better To Give

Christmas was fast approaching as to what our plans were going to be for the holidays. My family was going to be nearby but Hades' tradition was to fly home on Christmas Day. We agreed to spend a couple days with my family then on the 25th fly up North so I could meet her Mom and siblings.

Before any traveling was to happen, we were deciding when to exchange gifts. When it came to presents, she couldn't wait and although I purchased her gift weeks prior, I couldn't wrap it until I was ready to give it to her. So one day, unexpectedly I wrapped it and presented it to her. She had yet to get my gift. My present to her was an all expense paid trip to a day spa where she would have her choice of treatments.

The day she we were supposed to drive down to my Sister's to see my family, she said she would need me to take her to go pick up my present. At her request, I dropped her off at her favorite book store, which was dedicated to the metaphysical, which was where she bought her Tarot Cards. After a few more last minute errands we went home to finish the gift exchange.

We were supposed to leave to see my family hours ago, so without further ado, I ripped opened the wrapping paper. I received a stack of self-help materials (books, affirmation cards, etc.), which included an encyclopedia on interpreting Tarot Cards and understanding relationships through a metaphysical approach. These books were for her.

She did add that we could use these books to have one-on-one at home therapy sessions so she could become more of a team player in our relationship. Of course these sessions never did happen no matter how many times I asked if we were ever going to begin.

Merry Christmas!

CHAPTER 71
The Ghost of Christmas Past

We arrived at my sister's hours later than planned. We were to spend two nights there, fly up North on Christmas Day, and spend four days with her family. Hades, for the week prior, was trying to back-out on the two day leg with my family. She kept expressing how my family was too critical on her.

On the second day, I ended up falling asleep for 30 minutes around sunset. I woke up to find out that during that half hour I had been gone, chaos ensued. Hades had just finished cleaning up a glass of wine that she spilled and was clearly upset. She pulled me into our bedroom and told me how mean my family had been about the situation. In her side of the events, my family teased and made fun of her to the point of tears. Now all she wanted to do was go home. If what she was telling me was true, I wanted to ask my family what they were thinking, but that was when Hades put a ban on me saying anything. Like she had already done with my friends, looking back now, I see this is how Hades tried to now put distance between my family and I.

Soon after this my family turned in for the evening and that's when Hades started doing shots. She pulled out a bottle of whiskey from my sister's liquor cabinet and by morning polished half of it off. To cover up the fact of her alcoholism, she, like a teenage girl, refilled the bottle with water. The whiskey was now a much lighter shade of brown, but still dark enough that no one would notice until long after we left.

We flew North to be greeted by her father and brother. Besides Dad, this was the first time meeting anyone else in her family. It was nice to get to know her immediate family. I think as far as family members go, I enjoyed the energy and personality of her sister the most. She was going through a separation from a cheating husband and with smiles and lighthearted conversation she put on the biggest mask. With Hades, I knew that mask well and, in that, she felt the most accessible during my time there.

The family still mourned the loss of her brother, which was endearing yet heart-wrenching at the same time. His presence was still strongly felt through the home through pictures, memories, and an uncompleted grieving process. Had I been there or not, the the old videotapes would still have come out. The ghost of Christmas Past made it all that much harder to accept that Hades would use the fallen brother's name to vow honesty, when she was lying.

CHAPTER 72
Smile

Hades took charge of getting our engagement photos done and found us a wedding photographer that was willing to work for trade as he needed less wedding and more engagement in his portfolio. It was a good deal so a day and time was set to meet at in downtown Los Angeles.

As was now very standard, of course we arrived late, about an hour this time, but what was different now was Hades decided to blame me for our tardiness. As the photographers set up and told us where to stand and what to do, Hades carefully nursed her Vitamin Water and when I asked for a sip, I found it to be about 90% straight Vodka. This wasn't the first, nor the last time I would unsuspectingly get a mouthful of alcohol when I was expecting quite the opposite. I guess by now we had entered the "shame on me" milestone.

Within about 30 minutes of photos being taken, Hades slowly transformed into her more than tipsy self and was requesting to get a shot completely immersed in the water of the fountain. After finally convincing her that being soaked head to toe would end the shoot all together, she backed off of that idea.

Instead she decided to walk on a ledge which on the other side had what looked like a 6-story drop. My hands still sweat thinking about her walking in her 4" heels on this ledge when she couldn't even sit atop her balcony without going to the hospital. This fall would have been fatal.

The drunker she became the more annoyed the photographers would become and as the sun finally set we called it a wrap. The photos themselves would come out wonderfully and as the photographer would head home to check out the results, I was left with a Hades that was hungry and starting to sober up.

One thing to know about downtown L.A. is when the Concert Hall is closed, many of the restaurants around it are as well. As I tried to find Hades a place to eat, her Borderlineness was kicking in. I watched her eyes go from "I love you forever," to "die in a fire" as she pulled things out of thin air to start a fight.

If there had been no traffic, we probably would have arrived home, fought a bit more and went to bed in silence. However, since I-10 was bumper to bumper, I had no choice but to find the nearest restaurant and order up a Margarita to ease her Borderline nerves into submission.

CHAPTER 73
Coupling

After the great *We Need To Talk* incident Hades agreed to go to couples counseling on top of our own individual therapy. I reached out to my therapist, who knew her therapist and they came up with a name of someone that they thought would be good for us. She was a younger therapist still going through training and when we arrived to fill out paperwork, Hades learned that this therapist was under the guidance of her own. She started to freak out. That was something, at the time, I didn't understand. Most of what would happen in our sessions here, I would volunteer to my own therapist, but Hades was like a deer in headlights. It was only later I realized that Hades reacted as she did because she was probably telling her therapist her own altered reality, and now that could be shaken up as our conversations here and anything she or I divulged would go to her therapist. Her world was crumbling and she would later find a weak excuse to stop therapy all together.

After our first session we were given a homework assignment of taking each other out on a date. I saw this as an good start to ease into the problems, especially that of honesty, I really wanted to get out of this.

Instead of a date, we decided to create a full day for the other. Her date was first and I hoped to make a great day for her. It started by letting her sleep in. As she was in her slumber, I ran out to get supplies for her day. The pinnacle of her day was an art class. I found an art school that conducted a 4-part series on Saturdays. For a fee they allowed us to sit in on the first class. The unfortunate part is they give you a list of everything you need for all 4 classes, so to be prepared, I had to go buy everything on the list in multiples of two.

I surprised her with breakfast in bed which was nothing more than a breakfast sandwich from Starbucks and a drink, but that was typically what she craved when waking up. We then made our way to the 4-hour art class where we learned how to oil paint. Hades was so pleased with the class, and since we had all the supplies for all the classes, I signed us up for the remaining three. We would never return.

Afterward we had a nice dinner and headed home. It was still her day, so while watching a movie she complained about back pain and her inability to track down any Norcos. Once Famous Video Vixen was out of town and no one else Hades used had any narcotic level painkillers. As her dependency grew so did the intake of alcohol. It was these moments that I could see the Borderline within trying to break free and I volunteered to go to the office to pick up the non-narcotic painkillers she left there. During these moments, any excuse to get out of the house was a good one.

When I returned, she said what I brought back were not going to be enough, so she had our dentist paged at 2am to complain of "tooth pain" from her visit a few days prior. He then called her in 10 Vicodin. Upon popping three in her mouth, she was soothed enough to fall asleep on the couch while I went to bed.

The following Saturday she planned my day which would start well and end well, but would become very shaky in the middle. I enjoyed the day but on the way to dinner she revealed to me she forgot to bring the tickets to the event. Instead of skipping dinner we made a quick stop at Kinko's where she would have a mini-freak out when she had problems finding the confirmation email. Finally on the way to the show, she complained that we were going to be late and there was probably no point in going at all. That started to turn south when she finally wore me down and I offered to just go home so she accused me of trying to ruin the evening.

There was an hour or so that I thought the night was going to turn into a giant Borderline mess, but happily and thankfully, it ended on a high note. Although on the way home, we had to stop by the pharmacy to pick up a refill of her Vicodin for her "tooth pain."

CHAPTER 74
365 Days of This

Our one year anniversary was fast approaching. I know, so far all these stories happened in the span of one year. After the six-month anniversary incident, I feared what might be up Hades' Borderline sleeve. She had no auditions, readings, meetings, or anything industry related that might set her on edge. I wondered if we could possibly, actually have a celebratory anniversary.

Hades stayed home that day and when I arrived home she was in the shower. We had several good nights having dinner at Benihana, so we decided it would be a good place to celebrate. We had a reservation and Hades was actually on time. So far, so good.

Dinner was good. Hades didn't get drunk. Borderline Personality stayed in check. I gave her a gift which was more on the homemade side. I went around town and took pictures of all the places that meant something to us as a couple: restaurants where we first ate, places we have wonderful moments, the spot where I proposed and complied them all into an album.

After she opened her gift, she handed me a card which inside had a note which thanked me for putting up with her for an entire year and how thankful she was to have me in her life. There was also a note telling me she was going to buy me a Kindle. The gesture was nice and I told her the gift was unnecessary, but she was adamant. I have to admit, after sacrificing many things that I wanted while in this relationship, it was really nice to see her giving back.

Six month and twelve month anniversaries were like night and day. It was the next day where Hades reality made a visit. As promised she offered to order me a Kindle which cost her a little over $200. Again, I was really excited to have one.

About an hour later, I walked into her office to see what she was up to. She told me she was jealous. She was jealous of the present she bought me and now was looking to buy herself something. She was looking at a $1,800 camera. Remember, Hades was laid-off about three weeks after we started dating, which meant her year anniversary of being jobless was coming up. The only income she had coming in was her unemployment, which was only happening because I kept on top of the forms she was required to fill out and turn in. All she had to do was sign them when I put them in front of her. Now she was jealous of the gift... that she bought me.

I told her that we should discuss the purchase but less than an hour later she placed her order and the camera was due to arrive within the week. She told me she would use the camera to make money as a professional photographer and sell off anything she could to fill in the huge hole she now had in her bank account.

I was distraught. I had been working so hard to cover her bills, allow her to find herself professionally, negotiate and keep current all her medical expense payment plans, and save her home from foreclosure. And here she was, taking every penny she had at the time to buy a camera because she was jealous.

CHAPTER 75
Crack Pipes

But extreme fluctuations and temperature changes
Have been known to crack pipes...
...crack pipes...crack pipes...
             - Sage Francis

It was a random night and some important papers I needed for work somehow became mixed in the mess that was now my home. There was stuff everywhere and no amount of the work I did could keep it clean. I spent most Sundays scrubbing the carpet in the dining room because it was the one place Hades really didn't work or pass out, therefore it became a sanctuary of cleanliness.

As I was digging through piles of clothing, papers, and trash that littered the bedroom, I found a small bag probably for cosmetics. I opened it and inside I found a small glass pipe, a lighter, and a half dozen empty baggies. This bag was something Hades had bought after we met, which meant these pipes had been used. For what, I had no idea. I still gave her the benefit of the doubt, went out to the living room, and calmly asked her what these were. Hades gave me the best poker face she could and said, "those are old."

"Can I throw it away?" I asked. When she said it was okay, that meant one of three things: 1. It was old and she didn't need it. 2. She could easily find another. 3. There was another in the house. I threw the pipe, bag, everything into the trash. I'd be lying if I didn't say I was keeping an eye on it to see if she would try to sneak it out. In the meantime, I kept searching for my paperwork and now more paraphernalia.

In the bathroom, she had tote bags hanging on the wall. In one of them was a small bag with a monkey face on it. To anyone else, it might have looked like a memory from her childhood, a keepsake or reminder of the innocence of her youth. However, to me, it was out of place. I looked inside and here found another pipe, a lighter, a couple empty prescription bottles with Whacked Out Neighbor's name on them, and more empty baggies. It now made sense why a non-smoker would buy so many lighters.

Like a bad 80's cop show, I dipped my finger into a baggy and tasted it. I had no idea what it was, but it was bitter. I assumed it was Speed since she mentioned smoking it before and "snorted two lines of it" the night before her first seizure. What was most troubling was how she admitted that smoking Speed is one of the worst things you can do, as it will literally rot your brain.

This time I would have to be more discreet. I wanted to know if she was using and confronting her with this would just lead her to lie to me even more. I needed proof. I left it there and laid the monkey face in a way that if it was disturbed, I would know. But that wasn't enough, she could always say she just moved the bag and the pipes were old. I also drained the lighter so if the bag was disturbed and if a new lighter appeared, I would have my smoking gun.

CHAPTER 76
Speaks for Itself

hades   Inbox | x

to me   show details 12/21/10   Reply

I was in this whole scene during the time you write about. Your not using names but I know of everyone you write about. Thought I should tell you the nude photographer guy was my boyfriend and we were living together when these photo shoots happened, this hades was giving him BJ's and having sex with him during and after the photo shoots, that was why ffprmf and hades were fighting, it broke us up and i moved out all because of hades. I know for a fact she had sex with, not just kissing, Joey the thug(HIV+), the artist guy, the hairdresser, the tattoo guy, the whacked out neighbor, white trash actor, 3 of clubs guy, nearly every guy around her was doing her. Probably still are, plus a whole new bunch. I'm no angel, I slept with some of these guys too, I'm no longer in that scene. Your not the only one selfish hades screwed over. Count your blessings and get yourself checked for something you can't wash off.

Reply   Forward

CHAPTER 77
East Coast Friend

Hades, as it appeared, was most likely still using much more than I knew about. She made it clear that she needed occasional Xanax and pain killers like Norco to get through the day. At times I would find plates on the floor with, the cliched rolled up dollar. She would say it was Adderall, but now with the discovery of the pipes, I assumed Speed or worse. She did admit to doing Cocaine the first time we broke up, so it wasn't something I could rule out just yet.

I went to her East Coast Friend (ECF) to confide in. I called her and told her about the pipes and random baggies I found around the house. East Coast Friend and Hades had shared a bit of a sorted drug fueled past: Speed, Cocaine, Methadone, and even Ketamine. Hades told me at one point she cut off all contact with ECF for a year in order to slow down the drug use.

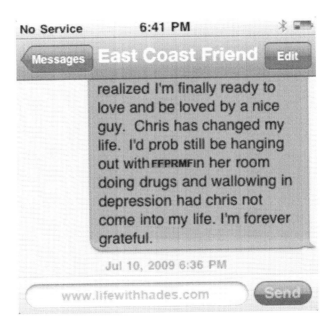

When ECF was visiting, her and I quickly bonded and besides wine, she not only admitted to being clean, but also appeared it. She seemed like the logical call to make and she was not only shocked that Hades was possibly using, but was supportive to figure out how to get her back on the right path.

It's funny how supportive ECF was to my concerns over Hades' drug use. It made sense at the time, as she was sober, and I truly felt she not only cared but also wanted to help. I would later find out that during ECF's visit, her and Hades were buying drugs behind my back from Once Famous Video Vixen.

Addicts are fantastic liars.

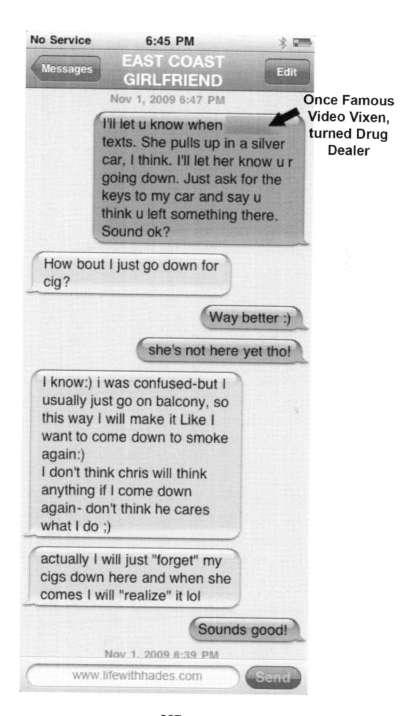

CHAPTER 78
Monkeying Around

Two days is all it took. She was on a cleaning binge, which usually happened randomly at 2am. I found her mopping the bathroom ceiling. As she scurried around the house, I went in and looked at the bag. Where the monkey was set up to be looking up at me, he was now face down, as if hiding in shame.

"We need to talk," I said to her. Her face went pale as her mind raced. I reached over and pulled out the monkey face. She was backed into a corner and then, and only then would she attempt to be honest with me, and even then she would dig deep to find what little lie she could muster.

"I just found that," she said, "and took the last hit that remained in it."

"I want to help you get though this," I said. I didn't yell. I didn't scream. I didn't point fingers. I had what I needed, proof that she was still using Speed, and now I wanted to give her what she needed: help. I told her how I found the bag a couple days ago and calmly said to her, "I'm not going to make you stop cold turkey, but we do need to make some decisions to move in the right direction."

She sat down and stared at the wall for a moment before asking me, "Where did you come from? How are you not mad?"

"How would that help this?" I asked.

I saw this as potentially a long road, but the first thing she agreed to was to tell me what and when she was using. Her personality changed depending on what chemical was coursing through her at the time, and I said that it was only fair to me to know which one I was going to be dealing with at the time.

She showed me her stash which she kept in a business card holder in her purse, she used this when she snorted it. The pipe hidden in the bathroom was for when she wanted to smoke it. We talked it out some more and eventually I went to bed. I woke up a few hours later and it was then she told me she was upset at how I tricked and tested her, that I should have called her out when I found the pipe instead of setting her up. I reminded her how I did that with the first pipe and she lied to me. We were now in Borderline territory and the argument was no longer about who was right, but how the situation made her feel.

It was here that while she did agree to keep her end of the "what was she using" bargain, but she was also going to stop going to therapy (both individual and couples). Logical or not, in her mind, she finally found an out to her therapy conundrum, and was somehow using getting caught in her addiction as the reason she no longer needed therapy.

CHAPTER 79
The We Dog

Borderlines like having pets. Of course, most people enjoy a cat, dog, rabbit or some other type of affectionate creature living under their roof. I have a dog but wouldn't consider myself Borderline. However, Borderlines, from the research I've done, seem to have pets for different reasons. When we started dating, Hades had a dog and two cats, one of which she attributed to saving her life. She told me, if I remember this one correctly, that she was visiting her sister and at some point during this family visit she decided to overdose on something... I want to say Ibuprofen, but that seems rather unexciting suicide attempt in the world of Hades. Maybe "over the counter" was all she had at the time. As she lay there, presumably dying, she thought about one of her cats.

"Who would take care of him?" she thought. It was this, most likely foggy, thought that caused her to call out for help and postpone the chilly hand of the Grim Reaper once again. I wonder how annoyed the Reaper gets with this one, false alarms constantly going off. The sickle can't be easy to lug around if it isn't going to come into play. That seems a bit heartless to say, but being one that filled her lungs with a life-saving breath on at least one occasion, I think I you underestimate how much I did care for her. I shielded her from Good Ol' G.R. a few times.

I've gone on a tangent, back to pets... Borderlines, at least in Hades' case, was not so much the unconditional love but more so the inability to abandon. Again, Hades feared abandonment so much she did all she could to push someone away. If you think everyone will leave you, and push them away, at least you will always be right. Dogs don't leave. Cats don't leave.

The first time Hades and I broke up, during my walking to work week, on a night Hades said she would pick me up, I, surprise, ended up walking home. While she was laying "paralyzed from anxiety" on her floor, we talked on the phone. Even broken up, here I was, feet on pavement, giving her a pep talk. In the midst of my courage inducing words, a cat ran in front of me.

"I want it," she said. I had little reaction to what I thought was a joke. "Get it for me," she continued.

"What?" I asked.

"I want the cat," she relented like Veruca Salt, "get it and bring it to me."

"It's not a stray; it has a collar."

"I don't care, I want it and I'll take care of it."

This conversation went on for about ten minutes and I think the cat knew because it quickly hid in a bush. There was a blatant disregard and detachment from reality. This cat, already meant so much to her, and in her pleading words for me to steal it, only made the reality that went on inside Hades' head all that much more bizarre.

The unfortunate part of a Borderline and pets is no matter how great the want and desire there is to have this living creature that will never, ever leave you; there's also a complete inability to take care of it. Her Beagle would not see the outside world had it not been for me. I spent a great deal of time trying to house-train the dog, but when she refuses to handle the poor dog for the "Mommy and Me time" hours she had it, it became an impossibility, and much like this relationship, I finally gave up.

There in lies the problem with the Caretaker that is within me. One day on a Petco run there were dog adoptions and I immediately bonded with a Mini-Pincher. It was improperly labeled, aged, and sexed and I asked her if she wanted it. That night, for $200 plus the cost of the Vet check-up and shots, we were the proud owners of a "We Dog."

The We Dog and the Beagle bonded immediately and now I had three dogs to walk every morning and every night. This relationship was already a 24/7 ordeal and for some reason I suppose I didn't feel punished enough as it was, so why not add another unhouse-trained dog. That being said, she was cute as hell.

We Dog was at first very clingy to Hades and she adored that so much. I felt bad for the Beagle at times, although still loved, the We Dog was like the new baby and the Beagle suddenly became a middle child.

I felt so bad for them when I left her. I wasn't able to take them with me when I did finally leave, it wasn't lack of want but I couldn't handle them all. The Beagle was hers before we dated, and like I said, the We Dog bonded so much with the Beagle it just didn't seem fair. I knew Hades would continue to be, as she called herself, "a slug," and the dogs would suffer for it.

Soon after I left she told me that one of them became very sick resulting in a huge vet bill. Thankfully before either of them died, her parents took them up North where they were given a yard and hopefully the love they not just needed, but deserved.

CHAPTER 80
Seize Her!

We laid in bed one night, I was dozing as she watched a movie. I'm not sure how long I was asleep before waking up to odd noises and movements. Hades was seizing on me again. A seizure is not a pretty thing to witness and since this was the trifecta of my experience with them, I had since read up on them. Seizures happen. The first time she had two in one night, which resulted in an equal amount of trips to the ER. This third one was a bit different in many ways. I had since learned a few tips.

The main rules are to stay calm and let it happen, move anything around the person that might injure them, and don't put anything in their mouth. I think I failed on all counts on the first one, even to the point of wedging my own fingers into her bite because I thought I was supposed stop her from biting her tongue. Apparently, even during a seizure, the human body is pretty aware of how not to do that.

The image of a Hades' seizure is forever burned into my head. Her eyes went dead, looking up and to the right; her hands curled up into her chest; while her top teeth clamp down on her lower lip as a guttural grunt forces itself out of her. For some reason I always thought it was best to do whatever I could to communicate with her through the episode.

Although longer, this seizure looked like the previous two, it was the after effects that were different. It took her much longer to become aware. After the seizure stops, there's this quick breathing, almost panting, to bring in oxygen, and while the shaking has stopped, the mind has shut down attempting to catch up with itself. By the way, I'm not a doctor, I'm only re-visualizing what I feel happens from my experience.

As I still hovered there talking to her, her eyes will eventually fixate on me. She has no idea what just happened and still for a few moments she has no idea where she is. Then, like the proverbial switch, her cognizant self clicks. Her eyes focus on me then dance around the room with a *where am I* glance.

"You just had a seizure." I would say as her synapses continued to misfire. She looked like she wanted to cry out of frustration but couldn't because she still had no idea what happened. I went into the bathroom to get her some water and when I returned she was standing in the middle of the bedroom, eyes wide. This is when the pure creepiness of this seizure resonated.

"Can we go for a ride?" she asked.

"Of course," I said, "let me just go get my keys." Then her posture and demeanor changed to that of a frightened little girl.

"But, *he's* out there..." she said.

"Who's out there?" I asked as chills ran down my spine.

"*Him.*" This went back and forth while visions of various killers and horror movie monsters danced through my imagination waiting for us in the darkened living room.

"Nobody is out there," I said still seeing pure terror hidden in her eyes. I went out into the rest of the house to turn on all the lights so she could see that our home was safe. When I returned to the bedroom, she was out on the balcony looking for some fantastical escape route. I put my hands on her, guided her out of the house in the non-jumping-to-the-concrete route and put her in the car.

We drove and drove until we hit a dead end. The close quarters of the car must have made her feel safe and eventually she returned to her senses. Once again her synapses were firing. Last time she had a seizure it was from Speed. Although I found her Speed pipes not too long before this, Hades would blame the lack of alcohol and her attempts at sobriety as the shock-to-her-system that caused this seizure.

CHAPTER 81
Mailbag

I always appreciate mail, both good or bad. I am also open to questions from readers who may be in similar situations. One of the original reasons for this book was because when Hades and I fought, I would hop on the internet and came up hopelessly distraught on the query "fighting with a borderline." With the exception of a few random posts about some ex-wife, there really wasn't anything out there. This book started as Dating a Borderline, which felt too clinical, therefore I thought I should just write this all out so others can see and maybe learn from my own personal experiences. Thank you, readers.

Hello Inbox | X

to me   show details   Feb 8 (4 days ago)   Reply

I just wanted to say "thank you" to you because I was dating a girl with similar character traits (diagnosed borderline amongst other disorders which she mostly denies) which already started to get me into stress, doubt and distrust. I met her over an internet forum and so far we've only had intense telephone-contact for a couple of months now. Always wanted to meet her but she delayed. I also witnessed live her taking an overdose of a antipsychotic medication after which I seriously considered cutting contact already - but it went on because I tried to understand her and feel for/with her. I'm also interested into psychology (albeit not studying) and believed that things might work out somehow. It's that voice/sweetness which kept me going on with her. Now she randomly doesn't reply to my messages anymore, keeping me wondering how she cannot respond even by text-message. I've learned through some net-research that she has a rather "easy" sexual mentality where she would display herself quite differently to me... Also noteworthy are her stories about her ex-boyfriends where she caused quite transborder scenes (for example, suicide-threats or inviting and hooking up an ex-heroin addict again).

I didn't read your whole blog but so far the this story is... pretty sick on her side. If you're displaying yourself truthfully there I have to conclude you're rather a "correct" person which should _absolutely not_ engage with her anymore in any way to avoid endangering your own mental health. Please take that serious.

You're really accumulating a story there - I guess it also helps you to digest everything that has happened. Maybe you should consider writing a real book about it? It could spawn a controversy which might be relevant in terms of getting it sold (if you care). I guess people want to read that somehow... Well, I'm no different, I'm quite curious. Although the most important aim for you should be to let go of her. This is no "hate-mail" but I also suggest you should think about the possibility of therapy for yourself in case you don't feel you can handle this whole "Hades-experience" by yourself in the long run. Stop attributing symbols to her and making some kind of science out of the relationship experience! Stop caring about it. Please find a way to - let those memories go.

Here's a link to a non-borderliner subforum which might be something for you:
http://www.psychforums.com/borderline-personality/topic46219.html (quality of forum not verified!)
Off course there are many others out there, it's just a suggestion..

I also found this: http://phoenixrisingaudio.net/item.php?itemId=26
Too bad I wasn't able to locate the appropriate pdf file..

Alright, that's all from me so far. Keep care of yourself.

PS: If you're putting this mail on your blog, I would ask you to blur out my email-adress if possible.
PPS: Curiously enough I'm an "INFP" myself (if this is a sufficient enough method to pin down a persona) but after a mental/situational breakdown I have been psychologically examined and tested negative on all personality disorders including borderline (I initially even thought I might have that). The only thing that might apply to me would be depression.

CHAPTER 82
All the Best

Well...you took the words out of my mouth D | x Inbox | x

[redacted] to me ← Reply

Like I said above, I understand deeply what you went through. I read your blog ravenously, literally consumed it one day, much like Hades consumed any drug on her horizon. I hope you are staying strong and away from the underworld she swirled you into. I must say it seems like a long road to recovery. I'm still battling with my breakup from my boyfriend from 4 years ago. He constantly threatened suicide, I can remember staying at a 5 star hotel and not minutes later he left unannounced and called me from the roof saying "I'm going to jump...you've made me know how worthless I am". Jump he didn't...like usual but the sociopathic behavior never stopped and was relentless. On one occasion, he came to my house at 3 am announced his father was dead and made me buy both the tickets for the funeral...it turns out his father wasn't dead; he had a very mild heart attack. He then proceeded to take half of his fathers pain medication and anything else he could get his hands on. The list goes on and on. I appreciate your blog and really hope others can learn that the only thing you can do is run for your life...and try to leave them with the cats. All the Best, [redacted]

← Reply → Forward

CHAPTER 83
Unpainted Corner

Hades and I had a deal. She needed help and although she quit therapy because I "tricked" her and therefore didn't trust the therapist that would allow that to happen. She had been looking for an out of therapy for some time as Couples Therapist reported to Her Therapist, which meant the world she was creating for herself would be in danger of exposure. I cannot even understand or fathom how she can get through her life day-to-day when so much of what she says contradicts with what she does.

Our deal, with we agreed to just recently was, Hades was supposed to tell me what she was using and when. Mostly she took Xanax, Norcos and topped it off with a bottle of wine, now there was Speed. Calling it Speed is being generous when, at the end of the day, it was Meth. It was most upsetting, but like everything else, it was something I thought we could work through. All I needed was honesty, but that was a trait and compromise that Hades was unable to give. I think I did my best, but of course there are always those *what if* scenarios I occasionally revisit.

There was one night she "forgot something in the car" and it was nights like this when she would usually return with a odd shaped bulge in a pocket. The most unique trait of Hades' dealer, Once Famous Video Vixen, was she put the drugs she sold in small containers that she then Bedazzled. There were dozens of this little one time make-up containers with various jewels glued to the lids littered around the house.

Tonight was no different when she threw on her white, fur lined jacket to run downstairs (it was this jacket that became the center of the "Hades can't pack" joke when it wound up in Hawaii with us). She came back, I tried to read her, a sometimes difficult task. We chatted for a minute about something, the jacket came off and landed on the couch, and she went out to see if Single Gay Guy across the hall was still home. I was alone with the jacket and assumed there was something in the pocket. I picked it up, and trying to give her the benefit of the doubt, moved to hang it up. She came back inside, her eyes slightly wider than normal seeing the jacking in my hand.

"What are you doing?" she asked.

"Hanging up your jacket," I said.

"Why?"

"You left it on the couch."

"Well... I wanna wear it some more."

I handed it to her, now 99.9% sure there was "shit" in the pocket. She quickly tried to control the situation by picking up her phone to call her friend's dad, a doctor who said he would help with her sick brother's mystery illness. As she was leaving a voice mail, she moved from the living room to the bedroom. I casually followed.

As she hung up, she moved toward the bathroom.

"Wait a second," I said. She turned. "Is there something you need to tell me?" Her eyes stared daggers into mine.

"Is there something you need to tell me?" she asked.

"No," I replied. "Is there something in your jacket I should know about?" Still silent she took it off and handed it to me. I didn't even have to get to a second pocket, as I found Speed/Meth in the first.

"I knew you went through the pockets," she said with a bit of anger as she tried to turn the tables.

"I didn't," I said calmly, "I just know you. You are a great liar but you do have tells."

And when she had no where to walk and no where to turn without stepping on wet paint, she turned to her last feeble attempt to gain control: Tears.

Hades once told me a story about when she was in High School. She lied to her parents and went to a party. She stayed out too late and as she drunkenly crept through her darkened house, she thought she committed the perfect crime. As she tip-toed into her room to pass out in her bed, "Hades," in her mother's voice echoed from the pitch black corner of the room.

When the lights turned on now it wasn't to a High School kid doing what High School kids do, but this time it was in the recesses of my head realizing I really had become the parent to my 29-year-old fiancee. Even if we didn't know it then, there was no going back. She depended on me and lied to me just like she did to her parents, pretending the whole time I was actually her partner.

CHAPTER 84
V-D

Valentine's Day was fast approaching so I planned for a two-day getaway at a hotel on the beach in Santa Monica. The best part was they allowed dogs, so I loaded the five of us into the car and headed West. Besides a Valentine's Day dinner reservation there weren't any real plans except relaxing, enjoying the beach, and of course some time in the spa.

We had dinner at the Sushi place she used to work. I met a couple of former co-workers as we enjoyed various dishes. Later we enjoyed massages and just had a nice relaxing weekend free from worries and concerns. Overall, these 48 hours are not very exciting, it's the before and after bookends that marked the beginning of the true end of this never-should-have-happened engagement.

Two days before we checked into our hotel, Hades was hired for a video shoot. She was cast off her photos and resume alone, which meant that she never met any one before she showed up on set. The video was for some, if I remember correctly, Middle Eastern pop singer... in other words this video would never be seen or cared about by anyone in the U.S. The great thing about it being geared for a Middle Eastern audience were the rules: no gratuitous sexuality; no touching. Fantastic from a fiance's stand-point.

During our trip, the Music Video Director reached out to Hades and said he'd like to discuss bringing her on for other videos as well as the Still Photographer when she wasn't on-camera. This was quite possibly a positive move for her career in photography and hopefully would start paying off that camera purchase.

We checked out of the hotel the day after Valentine's Day while she set up a dinner meeting with Middle Eastern Video Director. I dropped her off and she said she trusted him enough to drive her home. Four hours later she called from the car to say she was on her way home then immediately cut out. Subsequent calls were unanswered until she came home.

Her mood was altered and I don't mean that in a drug induced way, just not how a normal girl would normally act/feel after a Valentine's getaway. Earlier that day she couldn't stop telling me how much she loved and appreciated me and now she was again distant. I probed her a little and she redirected until she went to take a bath.

I laid there revisiting all the trust issues I had with Hades. They weren't subsiding, nor should they have been, and I feared they would never go away. I kept wondering what happened tonight. I tried to imagine myself married to a girl I didn't trust, and how the thought of living every day in anxiety was such a sexy cross to bear.

I would have to once again set aside my feelings, fears, and worries as she walked out of the bathroom saying, "I'm pregnant."

CHAPTER 85
[I I]

Three pregnancy tests... all positive. Two parallel lines, three times over... Hades was a triple threat. "Whoops," I guess is an understatement. Honestly, I wasn't totally surprised, as Hades was at least a week late. It took me back to that last time she thought she might have been pregnant, only that incident was filled with booze and more negative pregnancy tests. Well, if there is such a thing as fate, all my life's decisions, all those choices, and roads traveled all brought me to this point in my life. Now what?

We had been in an off mood before she took the first test and now she was just balled up on the couch barely saying a word to me. When I went out to talk, she said, "Now you want to just forget about all that other stuff and talk."

"Things are different now," I said, "who cares about that petty stuff?"

She told me she needed space and some alone time. I tried, but eventually went to bed. The next day, exactly one year ago today, I woke up and found Hades asleep on the couch. I turned off all the lights, tucked her in, and went to work. Hades and I had, in our relationship term, discussed children. Neither one of us wanted them, especially not at this point in our lives, so when she called me later, that was her mindset as well as mine. I apologized as I was sure her mind was racing and she apologized as well and said she'd "take care of it."

It wasn't until the morning sickness that the reality sank in. "There's a baby in there," I thought to myself one morning as she laid there sleeping. I told her before we did anything, we should schedule a doctor's appointment and have a real test done. We made an appointment for the next day and I drove her. The sole purpose of this visit was to confirm her pregnancy.

We sat in the waiting room, I asked her if she wanted me to go back with her. She said she felt more comfortable going back alone as she wanted to discuss her drug history and how to get clean. That seemed fair.

Hades returned and we walked silently to the elevator. When we were alone and with a slight nod, "I'm pregnant."

"Okay," I replied, "I guess we have a lot of talking and figuring out to do." In Hades' hand, she held rehab brochures and prescriptions: Adderall, Birth Control Pills, Xanax, and Pain Killers. Even just getting positive confirmation from a doctor, I still thought that was a very odd combo to give a pregnant patient. What was even odder was on the way to the pharmacy, Hades told me her doctor didn't even do a pregnancy test. Apparently, according to Hades, her doctor was satisfied with the at home pregnancy tests Hades told her about. Strange prescriptions aside, this was a giant red flag.

"Did you ask for a test?" I asked.

"Yes," Hades said, "she said I didn't need one."

I had been to countless urgent cares and emergency rooms with this girl and every time they did a pregnancy test. That time in Vegas where went from urgent care to hospital to hospital, each time they took a urine sample. With this, and the prescriptions, I knew Hades already made up her mind about the future of this baby.

While this was a new situation for me, it was Hades' third pregnancy. She had told me about the two previous ones she had with her Musician Ex-Boyfriend of four years, both of which were terminated. I guess this was just another mark for her and she used the doctor appointment to score some prescription drugs. Why not? She was already there.

CHAPTER 86
Rx for Trouble

We were waiting for Hades' prescriptions to be filled when the pharmacy assistant told me there was an issue with the insurance. I called and dealt with the HMO as Hades wandered around the CVS filling her arms.

A half an hour later, the insurance issue was cleared up and I found Hades, mid-phone call, sitting in an aisle filled with 75% off Valentine's Day merchandise. She was talking to her dad who was supposed to come for a two-day visit the following week and deliver Hades a car. This would be the second time Hades totaled a car, the same number of times her father found a replacement up north, and drove the 1,100 miles to hand deliver it to her. However, on this call, she was telling him that she may not need him to do that as someone was helping her find a solid used car locally.

As it turned out, Middle East Video Director offered up his services to help the damsel in distress find a car. This, from a man, that knew her less than a week. I had since investigated him a bit further and found that he was not only married, but his Facebook photo was of him and his infant child. Although that should have made things better, it didn't, and those red alerts that should have been going off since day one were now at full blast.

We picked up all her prescriptions and at home further discussed our options regarding the unborn. All she really had to offer was, "if we had the child," with her drug history, he would "come out with two heads and three arms." I still was really undecided on the whole ordeal, but I wasn't so quick to just close the door on all our options.

I continued to weigh everything while Hades went to take a bath. When she returned a bit later, we decided to pick up the conversation tomorrow and just relax together. We sat side-by-side on the couch as she texted away. Texting was her tool, as she had used it before, to keep contact with people behind my back and at this moment it didn't feel any different than it did in the past. I glanced over and saw Middle East Video Director's name on top and a few other key words that didn't quite make sense. Two of them being "lunch" and "tomorrow." I was once again metaphorically put in the closet, the light turned off. I sat there in disbelief and could have possibly gone into denial if I didn't witness her unlock her phone with a newly created password. New password, in my head, meant that phone was full of new secrets.

"Fuck," I thought, "this is never going to stop."

A weakness of mine in this relationship was always wanting proof before making an accusation. If I pointed the finger at her and was wrong, the Borderline repercussions would have been too much to bear. It wasn't until later that night, when I woke up at 3am, that I would, once again, have my proof.

I picked up her phone, entered the new password and quickly scrolled. They spoke of missing each other, earlier that night she said she was going to call him, he asked, "What about Chris?" and finally there was their rendezvous for lunch the next day. I put the phone back where I found it and some how, in a state of numbness, fell asleep on the second couch.

My rest wouldn't be long, as I awoke at 7am, Hades has since moved from her couch. I went to the bedroom, the door that was always open, was now shut. I went in and found Hades chit-chatting on the very phone that held the cross-the-line texts. Once I entered, I acted normal, went into the adjacent bathroom to put in my contacts and before the second one was in, she abruptly ended the call. I walked out, her phone on the floor, Middle Eastern Video Director's name still on-screen.

"Who are you talking to this early?" I asked.

"The car guy," she stated matter-of-fact.

"Why do you call him the Car Guy?" I asked, "His name is still right there flashing."

"Oh, that's what I keep calling him to my parents," she said quickly.

I looked at her sitting on the floor; her big green eyes staring at up at me. I went back into the bathroom and saw the discarded positive pregnancy tests littered on the counter. Calling her out never did anything, she wasn't going to change, and now I felt like I was in a game of mental Chess. I knew of the texts and even after I told her none of this stuff with the "Car Guy" felt right, she just hugged me and continued down this darkened path.

Hades was an emotional Terminator and she would never, ever stop. She was hard-wired this way, and now all I wanted to do was to see how she would react to my Knight to Queen Bishop Four.

CHAPTER 87
Doctoring the Day

It was the day of the secret lunch between Hades and Middle East Video Director and I just happened to have a doctor appointment that morning. Fate was on my side. My doctor was close to the house in the opposite direction of the office. After my morning appointment, since I would pass by the house anyway, I decided to go home.

This came as a surprise to Hades and once when she would have been totally happy to have me home, now she was shifting uncomfortably.

"What are you doing home?" she asked.

"I had my doctor's appointment, so I decided I'd just work from home."

"Oh great!" she said with fake enthusiasm. A few minutes went by before she uncomfortably asked me, "Did you tell me you were going to be home today?"

"Nope," I said nonchalantly while I knew exactly the cover-her-tracks thoughts that were racing through her head. She had no car and an appointment at 5pm with an Agent I set up, so I offered to drive her. Her lunch was now going to have to be canceled. I sat on the couch where I looked through her phone the night before and worked away grinning inside as I made my chess move. As fucked up as this situation was, it was nice to watch her squirm for once. I wonder what she told the Video Director. She typically played sick, so I assume it was that, but he did know about me, so maybe she was actually honest with him. However, I don't think Hades knows how to be honest with anyone. Who knows, either way, her King was in check.

As planned I drove her to the Agent meeting and killed time waiting trying to figure out what my next move should be. Eventually I was going to have to call her out, but not until the time was right. Hades called me when she was done with her meeting, and I swung around and picked her up.

"How'd it go?" I asked.

"Not too good," she said. I assumed being thrown off her game earlier in the day meant she probably blew the meeting. I wish at this point I would have been chuckling inside, but let's face it, the reality of the situation was Hades was going down a dark path of infidelity... a path I'm sure she had taken before, but never did I have proof she had ever actually cheated. There were plenty of lies exposed, but no matter how hard I tried to prove cheating, I, at this point, only had circumstantial evidence. The glee inside of feeling like you have some kind of upper hand only lasts so long when you know eventually choices, from both of us, are going to have to be made.

"I got a job," she said, as we drove and discussed where to grab dinner.

"From the agent?" I asked.

"No," she said as she moved her chess piece into play, "from the Music Video Director."

"What's going on there?" I asked.

"Nothing."

"Something isn't right with this situation."

"He's just trying to help me," she said.

"This is weird coming from a guy you've known less than a week," I said. "Is he being professional?"

"Yeah."

"Let me see your phone," I said, "Just so I can be sure he's talking to you like a co-worker and nothing more. I don't trust this."

She refused, but I knew she would. I already knew what was being said in there. That's when she told me to pull over and let her out. So, I did, somewhere in Hollywood she walked away. There were many point of no returns, but this was the start of the big ones, where those decisions, both good and bad, where now going to be made.

I thought East Coast Girlfriend and I had some kind of bond and even if she was Hades' friend, she listened to my side. This was long before I realized she was sneaking drugs with Hades during her visit, so whether she was an impartial ear or a spy for Hades, I'll never know.

I decided at this point, enough was enough, it was time to know everything. While Hades was cabbing it to God knows where, I went home and for the next couple hours, I went through everything.

Everything.

CHAPTER 88
Pandora's Box

Hades hopped out of the car and I went home. I knew she wouldn't be back that night and I had no intention of staying either, but someone had to care for the dogs. When I arrived home, I finally decided to it was time to know everything, so I opened up her computer. Her passwords were saved for everything. I started with her Gmail account, where I learned that on the anniversary of her brother's death, while she told me she went up to Santa Barbara and might stay the night, she was actually hanging out on set in Los Angeles with White Trash Looking Actor and even had dinner with him.

I learned that at some point she spent some time with Hairdresser with the Horrible name and he said something along the lines of "it was nice cuddling with you again." Cuddling was the keyword used in the anonymous email I received before. At least I knew now it either came from him, or possibly, and I wouldn't put it past her, even Hades herself.

I moved on to her new email she was using for her Photography business and saw that the flirting with Middle East Video Director extended into some playful emails where they were now exchanging pictures. That was a newly set up account so there wasn't much there besides that.

Facebook was filled with a nice amount of random "When am I going to see you again" type messages from random guys. The best went back a little ways into around four months of our dating when she denied having a boyfriend.

I then looked in her Hotmail account which was mostly just used for junk, but looking back far enough I found emails from the guy she said was a Pimp. She originally met him based on some event he was hiring girls for, which then awkwardly transitioned into "That event was pushed but let's have dinner anyway for "selfish reasons." He added odd phrases like "You can always say no," and after their dinner said, "Let me emphasize... Thursday was VERY impressive! :)" What happened with him, is a mystery. It was a follow-up message that was enough circumstantial evidence to see she was most likely paid for sex that night she told me she had an interview. I hit print on that one and took with me because I knew I would never be able to look at her the same way again and if I ever did, all I had to do was revisit that email.

After that, I had had enough and started packing a bag. I loaded the three dogs into the car, but before I left, I grabbed her old phone. I had recently bought her a new one, so at the end of the day, felt this one, with the cracked screen was traded in for the new one.

From: **HADES**

To: **PIMP**

hey, not sure if you got my texts but every time i call it says your not accepting calls. i want to work thursday. i really need the money and i know i'll make this guy happy, even if he isn't the most desirable client, as you said.

my girl could too but you know me, and know i can do a good job.

call me!!!!

xoxoxo

Windows Live™ Hotmail®...more than just e-mail. See how it works.

CHAPTER 89
Pandora's Phone

I laid in the dark, on my friend's couch, three dogs taking up every inch on and around me. I had been venting the past hour or so and, at this point, was physically and emotionally drained. I pulled out the iPhone and looked at the broken screen. I thought about Halloween, the night she dropped it and how easily the screen cracked. Even with the shattered piece of glass on top, the LCD and touch screen worked just fine. I slid the virtual lock and entered in Hades' password. I felt I had already made contact with her event horizon earlier that night, so escaping this black hole named Hades was now impossible. I had no choice but to go deeper.

I found lies, deceit, drug deals (both buying and selling), back-stabbing, but most importantly, I found this...

No Service   5:47 PM

Messages   **White Trash Looking Actor**   Edit

Aug 31, 2009 2:39 PM

> Hey, I know this is an impersonal format to discuss this with you, but I feel like its easier to be straight foreward. Anyway, I've been really confused about our relationship since we talked last thursday. I've been thinking a lot about it, and it's kinda been driving me nuts. I care about you a lot, but I feel so much pressure to be more than I can be for you, and give more than I can give. What's fucked up is that it has nothing to do with anything you've done. That's what makes it worse, because it just comes off like I don't like you. Which is so not the case. I have genuine love for you, but for whatever reason, I feel like I need to take care of you. And right now, that seems to be consuming me, because I can't take care of you. I feel like it's only fair for me to be honest with you about this and let you know where I'm at. I think the best thing for me right now is to just be your friend. Otherwise, i'll continue to create wierd pressure in my head and potentially ruin any chance of us being friends at all. I'm sorry I'm crazy. :)

⬅ White Trash Looking Actor

Hades ⬇

Aug 31, 2009 5:28 PM

> I knew this was was coming when u said u dont like labels...I've used that one b4. Why did u ask me to be ur gf in the 1st place? And ur right it is a very impersonal way to tell me. It's unfortunate u think u have to take care of me because I dont want that nor did I ask that from u. Yes, chris took care of me but it clearly didn't work. I was independent financially and emotionally before him and will be now. I never even asked u for the $ u offered me. I wanted to handle it myself. I feel like u told me all the things u thought I wanted to hear (and why u would say some of the stuff u did just blows my mind), then once I started to really like u and we slept together that became unattractive. Was i just another notch? Feels like it- u actually texted me this. Kinda cold, dontcha think? Not something someone who truly wants to be ur friend would do.

The "last thursday" White Trash Looking Actor refers to was the night I was sick and Hades, instead of coming over to nurse me, she swung by, loaded me with NyQuil then left for four hours. The next day I boxed up her things and threw her out. Two days after I dumped her, so did White Trash Looking Actor, and he did it via a text message. As you know, and I learned this night, him and Hades had much more going on than just a friendship, and here she was admitting it on a lovely green background.

This was an eye opening night and sadly a necessary one. It's upsetting when your significant other can't be honest with you but a tiny little device will tell you, matter-of-factly, everything you need to know. I was glad I took the phone with me.

Besides, it allowed me to post all the wonderful screen-shots.

CHAPTER 90
Forked

The next day around lunch I left the dogs at the office and went home. I found Hades sitting on the couch, unbathed, just looking her typical unkempt mess.

I stood there still shell-shocked. I had bitten into the apple and cursed with flood of knowledge.

"You're going down a dark path right now and if you continue down it, you will lose everything," is how I opened it up. She just sat there listening as I went off on her. She started to deny things I knew to be true, so I just cut her off. I pulled her old phone out of my pocket and that's about when all the color drained from her face. It's so odd that someone that lies so much everyday has the hardest time destroying evidence. I couldn't have been the first to go through this with her, nor can I ever believe I would be the last.

"You slept with White Trash Looking Actor," I said more as a statement than a question. Backed into her corner she just nodded in silence. I didn't even bring up the prostitution.

Now she was choosing this path again. Hades reached another fork in the road, one way filled with sunshine as far as you could see, the other pitch black and somewhat horrifying. Like each time before, she seemed to be attracted to the dark because there's no commitment hidden in the shadows. Something about that draws Hades in, lifts her up, gives her an adrenaline rush. The darkness is one of her drugs.

"You are pregnant and you are sitting there flirting, planning meetings behind my back, and telling some guy you've known for a few days that you miss him. He's married man with an infant child. What are you doing?" She tried to deny again but I continued.

"I saved your house. I saved your life. This is how you repay my commitment to you?" I asked. "Your dead brother would be so disappointed in you."

"Fuck you!" she said. It was at this point she tried to kick me out.

"I pay the bills here," I said calmly, "you can't kick me out."

Eventually my hour and then some rant on her actually made her go into the bathroom and flush her Speed/Meth rock down the toilet. I wish it could have been a prouder moment, but she probably already smoked her high that morning and the move was just for show. As before, she would buy more and as before she wouldn't tell me.

After I said my peace, I grabbed some things and left her there alone. I spent that night in my office with the dogs. I left her with her cats. I wanted her to think about everything, if she was even capable of rationalizing that I was finally ready to leave her. If the darker path was what she wanted, nothing would stop her. But at least I tried.

CHAPTER 91
Dad

During this time, Hades' Dad was coming for a quick visit. He was here for less than 48 hours, his purpose to deliver a replacement car from the last one she totaled. A few weeks before I looked forward to his visit, but now it was potentially going to complicate things between Hades and I.

Not too long before this, Hades' roommate moved out. He could no longer afford it and said the mess she created were just too much to bear. The good news was this gave us an extra bedroom and bathroom, the bad news was he was pretty filthy as well. The bathroom he left behind needed hours and hours of work to just make it look presentable. However, this, at least, allowed me to reclaim a little bit more square footage into the clean side of things.

I prepared for his visit, cleaned the house, painted over the long forgotten dirt on the walls, and set-up the extra room to actually be a guest bedroom. To do this I had to scrub every inch of the carpet, put the extra bed together, and rid the room of years of filth. As I was running to Home Depot, painting walls, and cleaning as much as I could, Hades slept all day on the couch.

I was at work the day Hades' father was to arrive and just about the time he did, I received a panicked phone call from her about some weed that she misplaced. I tried to tell her where I saw it last, but she cut me off and eventually hung up on me. I told her to take her dad out to dinner and by the time they returned, I would come home and dispose of the lost pot. I found the baggie the weed was in, but torn up and littered in the hallway. Apparently her dog found it first and was probably mellowing out somewhere after gorging herself on dog biscuits.

After Hades and Dad returned home, I tried my best to pretend everything was okay. It wasn't, but being a quiet type he either didn't ask or couldn't tell. I asked him if he wanted to go grab coffee the next morning. At first he politely declined as apparently he wasn't a Starbucks guy, but after enough time, realized my offer was less about coffee and more about the talk that went along with it.

That next morning, I woke up early and as Hades' slept, her father and I drove together to the nearby Starbucks. It was here I opened up to him. I told him about Hades' inability to commit and her drug problems, the Meth/Speed I found, the pipes, etc. He internalized everything and told me how they had spent so much money on their other daughter's previous rehab that he'd probably have to mortgage their home to do it again for Hades.

I shook my head and told him that wasn't necessary. I already found a couple places covered under her insurance and would take care of the rest. He seemed thankful and even a bit saddened that our relationship was on the rocks. After the years of dysfunctional relationships, I think he saw how good I was for his troubled daughter. It was hard to sell out his little girl like that, but I knew that I was close to walking out and if I did, he would once again be responsible for her again.

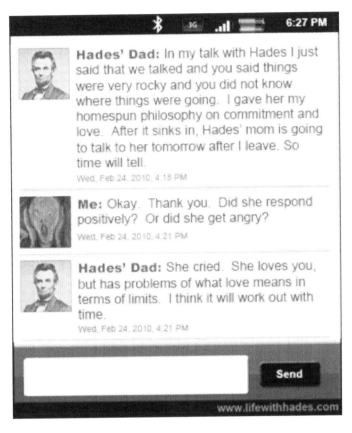

Later in the day, he sent me text message about their talk and how he thought it would all work out. That night the three of us went out to dinner. Hades and I pretended for, at least for the moment, that we were a couple again. However, the next day after her father left, the façade was gone.

CHAPTER 92
Long Weekend

I was facing the longest weekend of my life. Hades and I went on a 48-hour fighting marathon. If we weren't fighting, we just weren't talking. If I didn't resent her before, I did now and there was nothing I could say or do that would fix that. I now didn't trust anything that was coming out of her mouth. I was trying to figure out if I could leave, and if that was possible, how.

The fighting started when I returned Saturday late in the morning as Hades was getting ready to go. She had a photography assignment meeting with Middle East Video Director. If I didn't think it was over before, this couldn't have been any more than a read between the lines move on her part. If I screwed up as badly as she did, I wouldn't be running off to a meeting with this guy, I would have been home trying to fix it.

Eventually, she'd come back and the fighting continued. For many hours I'd sit in the living room while she was hidden away in the bedroom. I finally wrote out everything I was feeling in letter. I'm not sure where our letter communication began, I think she started it, but at times it seemed to help. The basic message was that I was not going to go through this again and she needs to address her low-self esteem issues if it caused her to go down this path of lying and eventual cheating. I can tell you she was not pleased calling my concerns "amateur psychobabble" as she went out the door.

Any time she left now all I thought about was who was she going to see. Had this been a healthy relationship, distance might have been helpful at times, but this deep in the rabbit hole, any time she would up and leave, all I could wonder was who she was leaving to see. I was desperate for something healthy now. I no longer wanted this psychological trauma I was enduring. Whenever she returned, the fight would continue and continue. I eventually called her out about not getting a pregnancy test from the doctor and why she wouldn't push for one. Deep down I knew she didn't even bring it up. Hades had a goal at that doctor's visit and it wasn't to confirm fertilization. I was tired of things not making sense and mid-fight at around 4am, I went to the spare bedroom and fell asleep.

At 7am I woke up to find her writing a 12-page, inked in red, note.

> Chris-
>
> *I'm only writing this instead of telling you because I don't want to wake you up, and yet I fell although it's important for me to get it out now, I'm not going to get you up so we can fight more. I've been thinking all night about your "Get Out of Jail Free Cards" & have to point out an example that supports my theory in that they can't exist w/ you...you have such animosity towards me about the face I didn't push for a blood test when the Dr. kept telling me I didn't need one from her. I'm sorry if I was*

weak there, but she really made me feel like I'd be pushing it by insisting on one. Though you did not specify a "Jail-Free Card" here, I am baffled as to why you can't let it go that I made a mistake there. You are so angry about it, & to be honest, I feel like you should be as understanding as if you did "grant" me a card. It has bothered & kept me up all night trying to figure out why you erupt so scarily when this topic is brought up. Because of your initial & subsequent similar reactions, I feel very alone in this abortion process. Why would I bring up a situation you get so, so mad at me for? You say you're mad at the Dr., but I'm the one who feels the animosity <u>you won't let it go</u>...and when I try to explain how I feel let down, it keeps coming back to this, & how I fucked. up.

And yes, I did fuck up by not being more adamant on getting a blood test right there. I was feeling a ton of overwhelming emotions @ that time, especially having to reiterate to the Dr. how much, what kind & how ashamed I was to admit what drugs I'd ingested since conception. I felt guilty, worthless and just wanted to take her advice & get an abortion asap. It's a terrible place to exist, emotionally, & I haven't been able to shake it. A huge part of me never will.

I didn't think I'd have to explain so thoroughly to you what a piece of shit I am for not even feeling like I have a real choice as to whether I can even keep it or not...if I had a baby that came out w/birth defects because of my mistakes, I could never forgive myself. I really thought you might understand that on a certain level where you wouldn't get soooo angry w/me about the blood test. And then to hear you haven't take into account (for me) the pregnancy, hormones & emotional turmoil that follows, just really blew me away & hurt my feelings. You are so preoccupied w/seeking answers to your own ?'s that you neglected to even try to relate to where I'm at right now. It's all about how I'm fucked up, how your feelings are hurt & why I am the way I am. I haven't been able to express much to you because I've never felt so emotionally stunted & frozen from myself. I can't seem to connect w/my own head - I just panic & shake. That's not like me...usually I have some deeper insight and can talk openly about my issues, even when panicking. I'm just so low & not in tune with myself right now that I can't give you the answers you obsess about, unless you want me to make something up, which I doubt you do. I literally started shaking & freaking out after reading your letter and although it definitely wasn't the right emotion to react on, I felt extremely angry & defensive. I'm not asking for a hug & "let's forget about everything" kind of response. But I would've felt less attacked if you weren't and aren't so adamant on figuring out answers to your ?'s first, & then maybe trying to understand where I'm at, only as an afterthought & because I have to fight w/you to make it known.

So back to my original point...you obviously feel justified in doing whatever you feel necessary to figure out your ?'s even ones from when we first met. I'm floored that you asked me about that today. But I'm sorry that I can't give you answers to everything now because of my current emotional state. There are no real Jail-Free Cards w/you. You're still over-analyzing things from when we 1st met --> our 1st date. And you're so blinded by that you can't even see how lost I am w/in myself. I'm sorry for the lengthy letter. I've tried to express this to you, but I keep getting shut down b4 I can figure out the right way to say it. I'm deeply sorry for all the hurt & pain I've caused you, & as you wrote, often wonder myself how you can still love me like you do. I don't deserve you, & as I'm sensing you're realizing this more & more, I can't help but prepare myself for you leaving me. I can see why you would want to, and that makes me so sad but I don't blame you. I fear you won't ever truly forgive or be able to let go of the past, and your level of resentment towards me is scary high. I empathize w/your predicament, and I hope you can truly understand that. I mean that. But we have to be honest w/ourselves in that there is no true Jail-Free card in most relationships, especially ours. (& btw, I am just as guilty of that and know it). I'm rambling now, so I'll just end this letter by telling you that I do love you very much & deeply regret causing you so much angst and frustration. I don't know what will happen w/us, and that is so scary & sad & I know I'm the root cause of it.

I never meant to hurt you like I obviously have & hope that one day you can really understand that & accept my apology for everything negative I've cause in your life. I love you...
Love,
Hades

Apparently it's wrong to resent and ask questions when you learn of infidelity in your relationship just days before.

CHAPTER 93
Infidel

It was incredible how everything degraded over the course of two weeks. I shouldn't have been surprised with Hades' history though. To think we would have made it this far was a miracle in and of itself.

Here I was reflecting on everything, confused as hell, and with no recourse but to leave her. She was never going to change, people rarely do. I knew that when I left she'd just move on to the next sucker.

I had way more proof than anyone needed, but until you are sitting in a spare bedroom weighing your options, it's hard to take the facts given to you and logically make a life altering decision. She was going to cheat on me again (if she hadn't already done so). Many would argue that even if she hadn't slept with this new guy yet, her actions and willful negligence was already enough. I not only had proof of what she had done but I had even more showing and telling me she was not going to stop.

We weren't really talking but when we did it was fighting. Even knowing she slept with White Trash Looking Actor she tried to justify it as "He lasted less than 10 seconds" as if his premature ejaculation was supposed to make me okay with everything. She later said "this is why you shouldn't go though people's cell phones, you find out things that you don't want to know." Hades really was the devil and after yet another argument I finally made my choice.

Hades picked a fight and then went to the store. When she came home, I went to her and told her "I'm done doing this. I tried and you've done everything in your power to make me leave you. I'll be out as soon as this weekend."

There it was. I said it. I did it. For the second time in our 14-month relationship, I broke up with her. This time it meant breaking an engagement, halting a wedding, moving out, and starting over. It was only two months ago her family announced in their annual Christmas letter their daughter was engaged. I actually wondered what they would write next year now that she was dumped again. As it ended there the entirety of this relationship flashed before my eyes. There were happy times, there were sad times and as I realized just how strong I was, Hades collapsed into a flood of tears.

All I could do was go into the spare bedroom and shut the door. As upset as I was, watching her cry was really hard. I was a bit in shock as to why. I warned her that this would happen if she kept going down the path, yet even with fair warning, she continued through the looking glass as if there were no repercussions to her actions. This was not a girl that was used to being dumped and here I was, someone that did it twice.

After an hour or so sitting alone reflecting on how quickly I could move out, I went out into the living room and found Hades curled up in a ball, sobbing.

"Why are you crying?" I asked, "isn't this what you wanted?" She was quiet. "You did everything you could to push me away."

"Leave me alone," was all she could say. I went back into the spare bedroom, and started planning my departure.

CHAPTER 94
Take Notes

I stripped Hades of all her power. I was finally prepared to leave and now she was going to lose everything. I warned her. Then, I warned her again, but my threats, apparently, where just that... threats. Now she was scrambling because my leaving meant she was most likely going to lose her home, her security, all her payment plans were going to go unpaid, which meant she was most likely going to move back home. Her world, that I was such a part of, was about to crumble around her.

As I stayed hidden in the solitude of four empty walls of the guest room, I received the following message:

◂ Back to Messages | Mark as Unread | Report Spam | Delete

Between You and **Hades**

March 2, 2010 at 9:21pm Report

hey chris,

it's so strange that i'm writing you a message on FB when you're only a few feet away from me, but as that seems to be how we're communicating right now, i guess this is the best way.

wow... i never saw the end of us coming- here, now, and especially like this. it's an understatement to say i'm devastated, but i understand where you're coming from and want you to know that i loved, love and will always love you. i obviously make you miserable, and i feel awful about that. i sincerely want you to be happy in life, and as we're both in such negative places right now, i get why you don't want to be with me anymore.   Middle East
                                                             Video Director

but one thing does bother me a lot: it seems like you truly believe that i cheated on you with   , and that makes me really sad because i didn't. i am upset you went to my father (which means my mother), my friends (- which means everyone else he and i know) and whomever else i don't know about yet, because you really did jump the gun on that one, and it has made this private situation between us, suddenly a public one. and now i'm dealing with people i shouldn't have to. most importantly, i can't go to my parents for support, and i could really use that right now, as i'm feeling totally alone. you are very big on honesty, but you're hypocritical at the same time; most recently, because of how you planned on deceiving me by lying about why you took my dad out and what was said. that really hurts and frustrates me because you live by a double-standard. and you seem completely at ease with your actions because of your reasoning behind them, just like how you feel validated about going through my private things. you can't explain away everything, especially relationship stuff, with logic though. it just doesn't work that way. i keep finding out more and more about what you've said to my friends, my parents- even today, and that is why i got so angry last night before i left. it's like how you say you just don't want any more surprises. i can honestly say i understand where you're coming from now.

with that said~ did i flirt to secure a job? yes. was that wrong? yes and no. we obviously have opposing opinions when it comes to that topic, so i can't completely satisfy you by saying i agree completely with your side; however, upon reflection, i can see now how much i was hurting you, and for that, i am truly sorry. because of that, i can now admit that i was in the wrong. but i was so adamant that i was right, and my blinders kept me from seeing much else. i hope you can one day accept my apology for causing you so much pain— for that and everything else you've had to put up with.

as for my behavior during these past few weeks, i have reacted strongly, immediately, and most recently, seemingly not at all (though that's not really the case), and i hope that you can take into account the fact that being pregnant has worked against me, physically and especially emotionally. i don't even feel like me at all right now. i'm not trying to blame everything on being pregnant, because that would be wrong, and then i would fail to face the mistakes i've made with us. but i am dealing with a lot more than i'm used to, and in addition to the loneliness that goes along with the current situation between us, i feel like i'm on an emotional roller-coaster i can't get off of. i know that as a male, you can't fully understand what i'm talking about, but maybe someday down the line when you're not so angry with me anymore (hopefully), you can take some of that into account.

i didn't start this letter with a solid point in mind so i'm sorry if i don't address all your questions at once. i just needed to get some things off my chest, so there they are.

with love,

Hades

Finally she admits to a few things, especially the "flirting" which later I of course find out was much more than casual flirting. Even at this point she was telling Middle East Video Director she couldn't wait to have him over so she could cook for him.

It's my understanding that a Borderline will use any and every avenue to gain control of an emotional situation. One tactic they typically employ is that of guilt. Here you see that she is using angles of how I've isolated her from everyone as well as her pregnancy to make me feel bad about my decision. She also throws in accusations of my "lying" to attempt to gain a balance as I was, especially now at this point, always calling her a liar.

This note didn't phase me and the conversation afterward didn't yield the results she wanted, so the next morning when I woke up and headed to the guest bathroom to get ready for work, I found this:

Dear Chris

You are wrong about me. Maybe one day you will see that. Maybe not.

I wish I could explain what's happening with me, but as soon as you said you don't believe anything I say, I realized just how badly you want out of this relationship. <u>I didn't want us to end, for the record.</u> You did...and that's obvious by the actions you took and choices you made to solidify the end of us. But you can't rightfully accuse me of being on the verge of ending us because I wasn't about to.

Do I know in my heart that I've treated you poorly? Yes- I didn't think of it like that before & it's a hard pill to swallow now --> and for that I'm deeply sorry. I genuinely do love you and thought you were my soulmate.

Do I need help? Obviously yes. I feel like a horrible person, and at the same time, I know I'm better than what you perceive me to be.

I never seem to be able to address what's wrong with you. It's all about how fuck up I am right now and instead of fighting it (like I've tried to), I'm just going to bow out... because I'll literally crack if we have another fight. I can't take it.

I really thought you would be there to help me, help us get through this. That obviously couldn't be further from what you thought, and I'll take the blame for that. I am so sorry for causing you so much pain and consequently animosity. But I do have to say that I didn't want this break-up. You did. And that's ok. It sucks, but I get it. I wouldn't deal w/me either. Every ex hasn't. I should expect you to stick it out when I make you miserable. But please don't put the end of us on me, as my choice. It wasn't. I love you.

More guilt layered upon guilt. All I could say to this one was to ask her how she didn't expect me to leave, when I did it for the same reason once before and warned her many times the bed she was about to lie in.

CHAPTER 95
Abort Mission

I immediately started boxing my stuff. Any moment I was at home either went towards packing or spending time behind a closed door in the spare bedroom reflecting on my choices the past year as well as my latest big decision. I moved into this place less than four months ago and here I was revisiting all my possessions, putting everything into boxes once again.

There was the small little matter of an embryo to deal with. This was my first time being in this situation, it was Hades third. As pro-choice as I was and still am, I did attempt to discuss our options. Hades however cut those conversations off as quick as she could. As evidenced by her doctor visit where she didn't even bring up the unborn child, it was painfully obvious that her mind was made up. Now that I was leaving, all that was left was the procedure itself.

She called and made the appointment and as I promised to her all along, I drove her there. The clinic was hidden from sight and you had to be buzzed in. We argued the entire way and sat in silence upon checking-in. There were two other couples in the waiting room. I wondered why they were there. Where they in just as bad of shape as we were? Where they here for the same reasons? Sitting side-by-side, Hades and I didn't speak a word, didn't touch, as important as this decision was, we were outside of ourselves, disassociated from the reality of the rock and the hard-place we so callously placed one another.

As we waited, the other two couples were called back. As we sat there alone, our seats shifted. We not longer sat directly next two each other, but in chairs perpendicular to one another. It was at this moment Hades started to cry.

"I can't do this again," she said.

"Then don't."

"I can't have a baby all alone."

"I don't know how to be with you anymore," I said, "but if you aren't absolutely sure about this, then let's leave." She sat there in silence. "I'll take you to right to rehab, right now. Then we can decide what to do here."

"Hades?" the nurse called out.

Hades stood up and went into the back room, but soon the nurse came looking for me. We were sitting in the pre-exam room. I kept pushing for her to leave and go right to rehab. We could revisit this in four weeks, but get clean and then make your choice. She continued to cry and asking the nurse for more time. Eventually time ran out, she asked me to leave and told me she was going to talk to the doctor about her options. I sat there waiting to be called back again when Hades started texting me how she didn't want to be a single mother. I told her again we could go to rehab but that was received with radio silence. About 30 minutes later, I was finally called back again. This time, I walked in to find Hades is recovery. The abortion carried on as she planned no matter what I was saying from the waiting room.

I sat down quietly on one of those stools with wheels. Had this been one of those other times I accompanied Hades to the hospital, I might have rolled around the room to try and lighten her mood. Things were different now, the laughter between us was no more. This relationship had run its course.

Hades: I just talked to the counselor. I can't bring a baby into this world without being in a relationship. I understand where u r coming from as far as not bein with me and I'm going to look at rehab centers tonight. But even if I went u might likely decide u don't want to be with me. And then I'm 4 more weeks pregnant. I know I wldnt be able to go thru with an abortion after having it inside me for another month. And then so I face being a single mom, and i don't feel right about having a child start off in a broken home.

Thu, Mar 4, 2010, 2:41 PM

Hades: They haven't done the ultrasound yet - I will tell u how far along I am.

Thu, Mar 4, 2010, 2:42 PM

Me: I think you should go to rehab tomorrow am. I'll take you. Wait to decide on an abortion until you are clean and have gotten therapy.

Thu, Mar 4, 2010, 2:45 PM

The Nurse kept coming and going, checking on Hades. I wondered what, if anything, she thought of us. This woman must have seen it all and another unhappy couple that were there only because we had to be was nothing new to her.

It was now time for Hades to go home and I helped her out to the car. She was still a bit loopy from the sedative. As we fought rush hour traffic we, for the first time in two weeks, weren't fighting each other. It saddened me that the only way we could have a discussion without venom was one where she was clearly under the influence. I guess that's what made it all work in the beginning, all the alcohol and drugs made Hades something she wasn't.

I had no idea who the real Hades was deep down. This one, however, was agreeing to rehab immediately, but as the sedative wore off, that soon went from "I'll go tomorrow" to "I'll go once I get my affairs in order." She took the list of four rehab places I had prepared before, back when I thought I could still figure this all out.

We arrived home and I did what I could as a once finance that was moving out in two days. Hades eventually made plans to go spend the night at Once Famous Video Vixen's so they could talk about ending a pregnancy. This was now Hades' third and she said that Vixen had been through a few of her own. Whether she was going there for the support of a friend or to do drugs no longer mattered.

Hades, as Hades did and does, was going to do whatever she wanted.

CHAPTER 96
The Calm Before

I woke up the next day and found that Hades had returned and crawled into bed with me. I laid there awake for an hour with her sleeping curled up into me. It was still Winter and a chill was in the room, which was silent, fighting was not filling the air around us. Eventually, I knew, as this relationship had, this moment would pass. I got up and went to work.

Friends checked in with me throughout the day knowing I was moving in less than 24-hours. Although I still had so much packing to do, I agreed to go with a friend to a movie screening that night. I found it hard to focus on the 3-D fad as I envisioned Hades sitting at home waiting for my return to what would be my last night living with her.

I drove home that night and as I pulled up to the garage around 10pm, Hades' car was not there. "Typical," I thought to myself. I went upstairs and began unhooking televisions and packing even more boxes. I thought I had rid myself of so many things four months ago when I moved in, but here I was tossing even more junk. The less I had the better.

I went into Hades bathroom to see if her engagement ring was still perched on her ring holder as it had been the last week. I was not surprised to find it gone. As I went to find something of hers to use as a bartering chip for the ring, I was surprised to find a small wine bottle laying on the floor with Sharpie marks scrawled all over the label. I had been in this relationship for 14 months now and if I had learned anything from it, it was how that jumped out as peculiar. I picked it up and at the bottom was a clear residue. I knew what was in there before I tasted it: GHB. Hades, within 24-hours of having an abortion, was again getting high on what could have been gasoline. Although I always knew it was the Speed/Meth, it was always the GHB Hades accused of giving her seizures. I became sick and consumed with not just anger but disappointment in a girl that was never, ever going to get help.

I packed with more vigor than I was before the discovery and that's when Hades finally came home. No telling where she was since I left her sleeping, but now she was coming home from the store. As she brought up groceries, paper towels and whatnot in a shopping cart, I continued to pack in silence. I don't remember who spoke first but the first thing I said to her was "What's this?" as I held up the small bottle.

"G," she said. I just shook my head and continued to pack. Then at some point I went off on her.

"You are worthless," I said in my rant. "You are a terrible girlfriend and horrible fiancee," I continued, "and remember how I told you how you didn't love yourself? I was wrong, you are the only person you love." Finally all the resentment for the cheating, the lying and the drug use finally popped. I was leaving the woman I wanted to marry and was moving out of what was supposed to be my home, I had nothing left to lose. "After tomorrow, I never want to see or hear from you again." My words were harsh and meant to hurt. As an addict, pathological liar, and cheater, I wanted her to feel them and know exactly what rock bottom meant. This was no intervention, this was me finally leaving a horrible woman with little feeling for those around her. This harpy, I felt, deserves to lose everything too. At some point, I stopped talking and she went to her room to cry. I hoped my words stung her like a thousand bees.

Eventually, in the middle of the night, I collapsed to the floor and sat there in a daze. Hades stood over me apologizing. "I am exhausted because of you," I said. As much as I was ready to leave, so many parts of me wanted to stay. If she even put in an ounce of effort I might have called off the move, the break-up, everything. Had she gone to rehab or tried at all, I would have stayed. I kept thinking about what my therapist wrote to me earlier that day as I wavered on leaving: *I have never seen anyone try as hard as you...she won't/can't do her part.* She was right, Hades would never change or treat me as a true partner.

Exhausted I crawled into bed and Hades followed. We laid there surrounded by three dogs and two cats like we usually did. We called this Tetris as we tried to be comfortable as every gap was filled in the bed.

"Don't move or we'll disappear," I said jokingly.

"We already did," was her response... and in tears, I fell asleep.

CHAPTER 97
The Storm

I woke up the next day and left a sleeping Hades to go pick up the moving truck. Upon my return Hades came out of the bedroom with her puppy dog eyes. By looking at her you'd think she wouldn't want me to leave, but she couldn't say or do anything that I needed to stay. All she had to do was ask me to stay and I would have. That's how broken I was at this point. Of course to ask meant she would have to do things to keep me. I knew she wouldn't. The night before she said things, apologies, and promises, "I'll go to rehab."

"If you were lying about anything you said last night, Fuck you for making me care about you," I said.

Two friends would soon be en route to help me pack all my belongings. As everything was loaded, Hades stayed hidden in her bedroom. She neither wanted to see the move nor my friends helping. As quickly as the packing started, it was finished. Originally, I asked if Hades wanted to keep any of my furniture but once I heard earlier that week she told someone I was using it as a way to stay, I loaded it all up. This included things I told Hades she could sell as a way to try and make her bills for the month.

Unfortunately time and space constraints made it impossible to load everything. I left a good amount of boxes and, as always, a handful of things I just forgot I had. And having a difficult time parting, I also felt a proper good-bye was in order. This meant the stupid decisions I was making wouldn't end just because I was moving out.

I went and checked out my new place. It was the first time I would be seeing it. Later that night I would go back to my old home. I kept telling myself it was because I left all my clothes but I knew why I was really going. We avoided the serious discussion and the reality that, even if I was there at the moment, I was gone. I spent the night and the next day, left early in the morning and took the remainder of credits at the day spa and went there to clear my head. I had the satisfaction of using up what was originally her Christmas gift, but other than that, it didn't make the situation any easier.

I spent the next couple nights at my place and the more I stayed away and the less available I was the more upset Hades would get. Random calls in the middle of the night asking questions to which I didn't have answers. I was still in a place mentally where I would automatically answer her calls, even if I knew I shouldn't. There was stuff of hers that I still had and there was still plenty of stuff of mine at her place.

One night the phone rang and she was demanding some of her things back. I told her I would be happy to oblige if she wanted to come get it. She refused and instead offered to meet me in the middle.

"Okay, I'll see you at 5am."

"What?" I asked. Things like this didn't shock me anymore. The 5am time wasn't because she was going to be up that early, it meant she was going to still be up doing whatever it was Hades did. "I'm not getting up that early to meet you."

"I want my stuff."

"Then come get it. It's here."

The more she pushed the more upset with her I would get. I started to bring up all the resentment I had for her until she finally decided to just meet me later in the week. I was done doing things at her beck and call and she was finally seeing that. Although I still loved her and wished everything could just change, they weren't going to, and the more I realized that, the more power I got back.

CHAPTER 98
Strangers

I agreed to have dinner with her to do a final exchange of the stuff she wanted. Clearly now, I wasn't thinking so clearly then. We met at one of our usual haunts. It was awkward at best, unnecessary at worst. In the middle of dinner, Hades got up to go to the rest room. As I sat there alone, doubting every decision I made the past year and two months, a voice from next to me said, "What's going on here?"

I looked up to see the couple sitting at our shared table looking at me. "What?" I asked.

"It's not a first date, so what is it?" She asked.

"Oh, we broke up last week."

"Why are you having dinner then?"

"I don't know," I really didn't.

"Who broke up with who?"

"I left her."

"That's good. You can do better," she said. It was odd getting reassurance from people I had yet to meet. Was it that obvious? She continued, "I have a friend that would be perfect for you."

Hades soon returned and our conversation continued. The couple next to us eventually left, but not before giving me their business cards. Obviously they wanted better for me, too. Hades asked me to go back to her place and again I agreed. As we both pulled into the garage, Hades was ending a phone call.

Earlier in the day I had lunch with her Aspiring Director Friend. He had become my friend in our courtship and we were working on a project together. I caught him up and he related to much of what I said as he went through something similar not too long ago. She asked me if I told him I was over her. I didn't remember saying that, if I felt that way, I wouldn't have been standing in the garage of her place... again. However, I did say the break-up, as painful as it was, was probably for the best. This turned into an argument and I immediately remembered why I shouldn't be standing in the garage of her place... again. I got in the car and left. Of course, the whole reason we were together that night, the exchange of property, didn't happen.

I went home, and was glad I didn't end up staying the night. I was sick and tired of her bullshit. I left it at that, but she couldn't take my abandoning her so when I didn't call her, she called me. The next night she apologized and said she felt bad that I didn't stay over. I had enough... almost... and for the next few days we fought over text and phone. She was working a job the following weekend and it was agreed while she was gone I would go collect my stuff.

Later in the week she told me not to come over but seeing as I had taken care of her home expenses for the month, I felt justified that I could finish clearing out my stuff. Besides, the We Dog had a follow-up appointment at the Vet that I wasn't going to cancel. When I walked into the condo, I understood why she didn't want me coming by...

CHAPTER 99
The Picture of Success!

I left her one week prior and while she was doing some promotional event (I would later find out that Middle Eastern Video Director was somehow involved in this) I went over to finish moving out. I still had boxes, clothes, and so many other things I just forgot I owned. Part of me thought she might be there when I arrived, but she couldn't let Middle Eastern Video Director down as I'm sure she thought he was her next ticket. I walked into the condo and was overtaken by a horrific smell. I cannot even begin to describe the mess... which is why I took pictures.

Seven days had passed and she was spiraling into self destruct mode. The place (except maybe the kitchen) didn't look even close to this bad when I first met her. Taking care of herself was clearly something she wasn't use to doing.

The Living Room was in shambles. There were trash bags littering the floor, everything you can imagine on the table and just crap everywhere.

To the right was the dining area that was always my sanctuary. While I lived there, Hades didn't do much in this area, so it was the one place that stayed clean. The carpet was generally scrubbed, the window was clean and the table was clear except for a centerpiece. Now there was a shopping cart randomly placed there.

The hallway was probably the cleanest area of the house, yet still littered with paper and trash. The door at the end on the right was a small laundry room, which typically was spilling out clean and dirty clothes all soaked with cat urine.

Compared to the first time I came over the kitchen was actually pretty clean. Looked like she was eating nothing but fast food. I guess she hadn't been able to have Middle Eastern Video Director over to cook for him yet.

The bags of garbage on the stove was a pretty nice touch. I guess fire is a pretty effective cleaning method. I didn't think it could get any worse but then I walked into the guest room....

Yes, that is feces, both dog and cat. I would have thrown up but a cat already beat me to it near the wall there. The house I once called a home was now a gigantic toilet. The more I looked around, the more I realized the shit wasn't contained to this one room. There were piles in every room. Onward to the Master Bedroom...

To be fair, this was a pretty normal sight of how it would look day-to-day. It drove me nuts, but I assumed if she could have one room to destroy, then I could have all the other areas clean. It didn't really work out that way. It reminds me of the time 8 months earlier when I was in there cleaning every inch of that room.

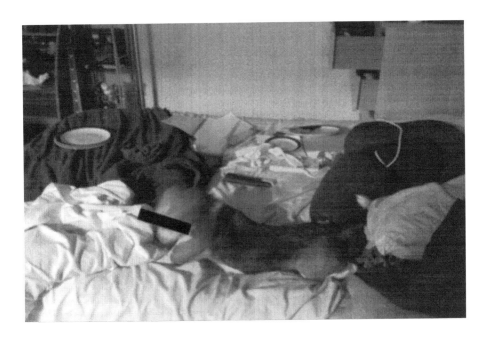

And finally the bed. It was covered in dirty dishes and steak knives. Fantastic place for dogs to jump blindly expecting a soft mattress.

This would have been hilarious had it not been for the dogs. When I went back the next day to get more of my stuff, it had appeared that Hades had no intention of returning this weekend, most likely spending it with Middle Eastern Video Director. She left dogs alone for at least 24-36 hours. This pissed me off so much that I called the ASPCA to report her for animal neglect.

CHAPTER 100
Cut the Strings

Even after all this, I still had some remaining things at my former home. Maybe it was just an excuse, but it was difficult to move on short notice, especially when you aren't taking everything under the roof. There's always something else, another set of items that was forgotten about. I thought I did a pretty good job of collecting and packing everything, but then I would remember that I missed everything in the kitchen. Add on to all this the emotional weight of a break-up, figuring out what lied beneath the harpy's skin, as well as sifting through a mess that resembled a war torn France.

I had left my keys on the last visit and there was so much animosity and acrimony that I just wanted to swoop in and get out, say good-bye and finally move on so I could start healing. I picked a night I figured she'd be home and just headed over there. When I arrive, her car was not there. As many times as her license was suspended, she continued to drive. I was disappointed because I wanted this done. I went to the nearby Starbucks, grabbed a coffee, and made a second pass. She was back.

I called her to tell her I was in the neighborhood and wanted to finish this. She agreed. She buzzed me upstairs and after she let me in, she went into the bedroom to either avoid me or sulk. I loaded up the last of my stuff and went into the bedroom to say the final good-bye. There she was, using the tool that always struck me in the lowest parts of my heart, tears.

Before I knew it, it was morning and she had handed me keys to her place. Like you are wondering now, I had no idea what I was doing. But there I was back the next night. We ordered pizza, sat in bed, and watched TV, but tonight was different than the last. She was distant and busy working on retouching photos. While silently working, she was also texting. I assumed it was Middle Eastern Video Director so I rolled over and as I dozed off, wondered how I ended up right here again.

At 4am, Hades climbed into bed, but not before turning on all the lights in the bedroom as well as the TV. The self-serving girl would never be anything but as I woke up to sight and sound. As fate would have it, she turned on Celebrity Rehab and moments after she fell asleep, there I was watching an episode that felt like destiny. Mindy McCready was laughing with Mackenzie Phillips and then fell into a full blown seizure.

That was all I needed to see. That dead look in her eyes was exactly how Hades looked each time. I played back this relationship in my head, again remembering all the time I took care of this girl, all the visits to various emergency rooms, urgent cares, and hospital stays. I thought about how I saved her home from going into foreclosure. She could barely take care of a dog, let alone herself or a significant other.

It was now 5am and for the last hour I was reliving that scared feeling I had almost one year ago to the day when I witnessed the first seizure. I turned the TV off, took a shower, did a last look around the house, and said good-bye to the Beagle and the We Dog with every intention of fulfilling my promise to her that I would take them away if she continued to neglect them. I sat down on the couch, picked up her phone and did a final check to reconfirm my always correct suspicions.

I was right. Well, that was that. And again, I walked toward a sleeping Hades, woke her up, and told her it was over. Again, she was crying but her gypsy tears no longer had any power over me. I tossed the keys on the bed and walked out of there for the last time.

I was proud of myself for this one. The only thing I didn't think about was that my car was in the garage. "Crap," I thought, "that didn't go exactly as planned."

I wound up having to stand outside her building for an hour until someone came out. Even sitting out there like an idiot, I felt a sense of control over my life again. It was a powerful feeling. However, this couldn't be the end. I had to make sure I didn't wind up right back here again, which meant I needed Hades to hate me... more than I hated her.

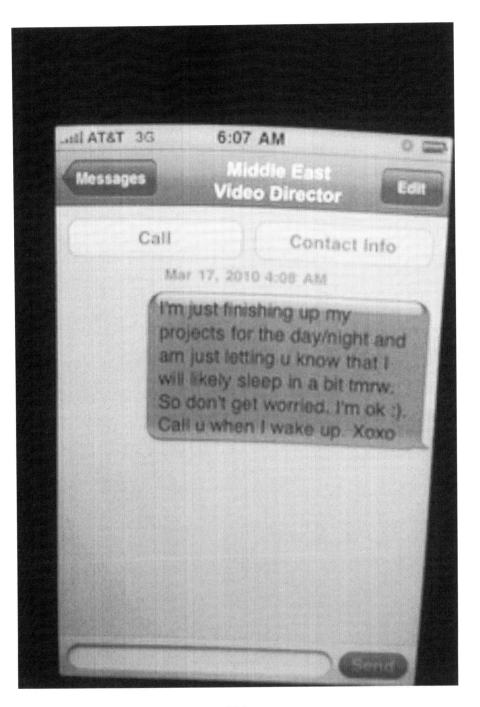

CHAPTER 101
I Am Over It

I not only wanted but needed Hades to hate me. That was the only way I was going to save myself. First things first, when I arrived at work, I tracked down Middle Eastern Video Director's email and congratulated him. He won the contest and his prize was a fully non-functional woman I was soon going to give the moniker of Hades. I was overly polite, gave him tips on how to deal with her at times, and finally told him (with a picture) how I spent the night at her place, which was something I was sure she hadn't and wouldn't tell him. My email was probably a little more jaded than it should have been, but my goal was for him to forward it to her. Which, he did.

Next move was to cut her off completely. She depended on me, and that all was about to end. This was something I told her would happen and now I was doing it. She probably realized this when she later woke up and couldn't access the internet. That was something I was paying for, so I canceled the service immediately.

Finally I canceled her health insurance since this was an expense I took over from her parents months before and now that we were no longer together, she could now be my dependent.

This did the trick as I would receive this text later in the day...

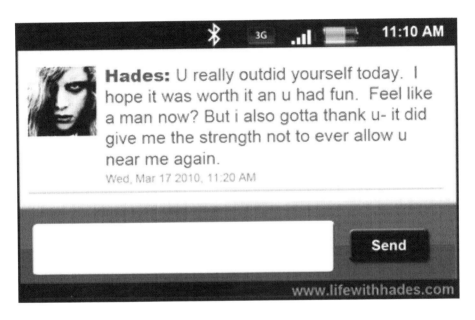

These continued throughout the day. Later, she changed from anger to guilting for a response, which also didn't work.

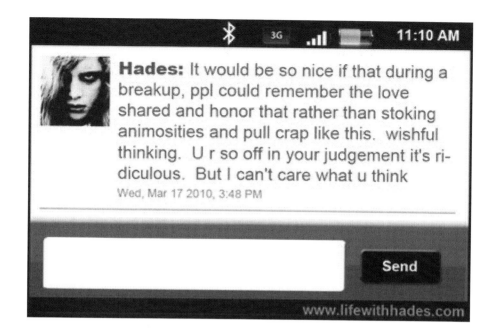

There are reasons people abandon her and it's based on her actions. Only a Borderline or Sociopath would do the things she did, cry "poor me," and still expect the wounded to look at the bright side.

CHAPTER 102
I Don't Float

After all was said and done, Hades was at a loss. I don't think anyone had ever left her like this. Maybe it was a lesson learned for her or perhaps she'd go on to make the same mistakes over and over. Hades went on to try to make me the bad guy. She accused me of stealing her childhood stuffed animal, random things from the house like vacuums, and even her father's CDs when we visited for Christmas. I was amazed that I could still be shocked by her actions and the choices she made for herself. I was more angered than hurt about the malicious label of thief she was giving me, but of course, she had to attempt to remain in the good graces of her friends and family.

Before creating this book, I thanked her sister for trying to warn me. I wished I had listened. To think I was supposed to elope just a day after that still makes me wonder just how infatuated I was for this poor soul.

This wouldn't be the end though. One morning I received a text from her dad telling me that Hades had suffered another seizure and asked if I would continue her medical benefits another month. It looked like if I wasn't going to enable her, she would make sure someone did. I agreed more for his sake than hers but in exchange he had to hear the laundry list of reasons why I left. This didn't seem to phase him really... I suppose he was use to it by now.

I would later see her again. She told me how her neighbor found her during her seizure and called the ambulance. This came across as yet another far fetched story and I was left to assume, it wasn't her neighbor at all, but any one of the endless guys or her next victim. Her fiance, only weeks later, had already been replaced. I wish I could say I was amazed, but I wasn't.

Eventually, I came to the conclusion that the only way to get Hades to stop lying to me, was to not give her the chance. It was at that point I cut off all contact. I stopped responding to her texts, her calls were set to go right to voice-mail, and I marked her email address as spam. I was finally done. It's not like she didn't try. Some days I would get numerous texts followed up by calls. She had finally lost all her power.

After a few months, the texts became more random; the calls less frequent. Her home was foreclosed on and sold to the highest bidder, and last I heard, she was forced to move back home up North. Although she told me she was going to remain single and celibate until she fixed herself, a friend of hers told me she was already hooking up with the next guy soon after I left.

Hades was and is still out of my life. Of course this doesn't stop the random emails I get from bill collectors looking for her, but at least I finally allowed myself not only the chance to get healthy again, but eventually seek out a relationship with someone that wasn't looking to suck the life out of anyone they encountered.

This was a surreal albeit a learning experience and hopefully sharing the intimate details of my life will help someone else out there aimlessly looking for guidance. As I said before, when I was in it, there were no real Borderline Help Lines, so if any lost soul is out there googling "dating a borderline" maybe they will come across this and realize they aren't alone.

There is a light at the end of the tunnel... and it doesn't always have to be an oncoming train.

Six months after we broke-up.

CHAPTER 103
Closing Credits

While Hades most likely remains the same, those in her life come and go. Here's a bit of a *Where Are They Now?*

- Middle Eastern Video Director not only borrowed money from Hades but also wound up in jail.

- Old Music Publisher Guy, who asked to remain nameless, told me directly that him and her very much had a physical relationship but never actually slept together. They did other things though. Gross.

- Both Wizrobe and her Musician Ex-Boyfriend both proposed to their girlfriends.

- FFPRMF met some guy, got clean, and moved out of this town.

- Joey the Thug went to jail and allegedly, while being HIV+, was drugging girls and raping them.

- White Trash Looking Actor's show was canceled, and although Hades blamed me for somehow blacklisting him and her from acting work, I like to think fate was just paying me back so the universe could once again even itself out.

Glossary of Terms

Adderall: Brand-name for a psycho-stimulant medication that increases the amount of dopamine and norepinephrine in the brain. Used by Hades to self-medicate and stay up for days at a time to "focus." Usually prescribed to people with ADD and ADHD. Can cause acne breakouts on the face if used improperly.

Balcony: A 15-foot drop.

Borderline Personality Disorder: A disorder in which a person never identifies with one particular personality type. Constant Splitting (Idealization and Devaluation) of those around you and can happen anytime, anywhere (see also Bear-trap and Mine Field)

Cell Phone: a tool to continue relationships unbeknownst to those around you.

East Coast Girlfriend (ECF): Old friend and part of the drug circle of friends. Hades side of the story is that she broke off all contact with ECF for a year to help sober up. Supportive confidant to me when discussing Hades' drug problem. Later, I found out that her and Hades were sneaking drugs behind my back during ECF's visit.

FFPRMF: Best friend until she turned on Hades. (see also Female-Failed-Pseudo-Rockstar-Musician-Friend)

G, GHB: Gamma HydroxyButyric Acid also known at the "date rape drug" made from degreasing solvent or floor stripper mixed with drain cleaner. It's used by Hades to achieve a 20 minute feeling of euphoria where she sits or stands there with her eyes closed and does a continuous "mmm-mmm-mmm" humming sound.

G'ing Out: The slang term for reaching the 20-minute feeling of euphoria.

Gasoline: Sometimes a form of this will be sold to an unsuspecting addict in place of GHB.

Hades: 1. In Greek Mythology, the name of the Underworld or Hell. 2. Nickname for the person this book is dedicated to (see also Sociopath, Borderline Personality Disorder, Pathological Liar, Harpy).

Hairdresser with the Horrible Name: Ex of Hades that wanted to take her on a fishing boat to gut fish.

Honesty: Not found, 404 Error.

INFP: The Myers-Briggs version of Borderline Personality. Example: *That girl is whacked, I think she's an INFP!*

Joey the Thug: HIV+ Thug that used GHB to subdue and rape women.

Lame Music Guy: Met Hades on the flight back from Vegas. Had at least one secret rendezvous with her.

Langoliers: The creatures in the Stephen King story of the same name that devour yesterday and the past. In the TV movie, they looked like meaty Pac-Men with razor sharp teeth.

Late Check Out: Something you learn to ask for when staying at a hotel because Hades is late to everything, including the standard practice of leaving a hotel.

MADD Class: Court ordered retribution for DUI.

MIA: Missing in Action, when Hades would say she was one place but was really mysteriously somewhere else.

Monogamy: A mysterious concept created by a man to control Hades.

Packing: Loading almost everything you own into one gigantic bag.

Poop: Piles to watch out for when walking in Hades' place.

Roommate: Scapegoat of problems used in order to get time away from your boyfriend.

Seizure: A reaction to drugs, which is typically very scary to watch.

Speed: 1. Typically amphetamine sulphate which is commonly only 5% pure. The remaining 95% is made up from other white powders, ranging from talcum powder and toilet cleaner. It has a very bitter taste. 2. A movie also known as "The Bus That Couldn't Slow Down."

Tattoo Guy: The guy that tricked Hades into thinking she had a job opportunity then asked to kiss her.

Ventura, California: City just South of Santa Barbara where Hades and I would go for quick and emotionally fueled getaways.

Whacked Out Neighbor: Addicted neighbor that would bum Adderalls off of Hades. Like Kramer, barged in without knocking, but unlike Kramer was not quirky in a funny way. Had little regard for others around him.

White Trash Looking Actor: Mysterious actor that popped up randomly but was apparently part of the drug circle. "We're just friends," Hades would say. Also according to Hades, she would never sleep with him because he has genital warts.

We Dog: A pet in the canine family purchased while a couple are together. Owned by neither and both at the same time. Other Varieties: We Cat, We Rabbit, etc.

Wizrobe: Former "Partner in Crime" who not just wanted, but desired Hades. Lashed out at her randomly when he realized him and her weren't together. One of the victims of Hades' insecurities.

Xanax: A drug used mainly to avoid confrontation. Comes in various doses, the "bar" form being the strongest. Example: *When questioned about possible infidelity, Hades quickly swallowed three bars of Xanax and passed out.*

101 South: The usual thoroughfare traveled when defying a boyfriend's trust.

61 Reasons Guy: Ex-Boyfriend of Hades that sent her an email listing 61 Reasons he is the perfect boyfriend.

911: Self explanatory.

Made in the USA
Lexington, KY
21 November 2014